SMALL CLAIMS COURT
WITHOUT
A
LAWYER

W. KELSEA WILBER

SOURCEBOOKS TRADE
NAPERVILLE, ILLINOIS

Copyright © 1992 by W. Kelsea Wilber

book may be reproduced in any form or by any electronic or mechanical ...age and retrieval systems—except in the case of brief quotations embodied ...hout permission in writing from its publisher, Sourcebooks Trade.

Published by:
Sourcebooks Trade
A Division of Sourcebooks, Inc.
P.O. Box 372
Naperville, Illinois, 60566
(708) 961-2161
FAX: 708-961-2168

Editorial: Ellen Slezak
Design: Monica Rix Paxson
Production: The Print Group
Cover Design: Concialdi Design

This publication is designed to provide accurate and authoritative information in regard to the subject matter covered. It is sold with the understanding that the publisher is not engaged in rendering legal, accounting, or other professional service. If legal advice or other expert assistance is required, the services of a competent professional person should be sought.
From a Declaration of Principles Jointly Adopted by a Committee of the American Bar Association and a Committee of Publishers and Associations

Library of Congress Cataloging-in-Publication Data

Wilber, Wanda K.
    Small claims court without a lawyer / W. Kelsea Wilber.
        p.   cm.
    ISBN 0-942061-32-2 (paper) : $18.95
    1. Small claims courts--United States--States--Popular works.
    2. Debtor and creditor--United States--States--Popular works.
    I. Title.
    KF8769.Z9W55   1991
    347.73'28--dc20
    [347.3074]
                                            91-28539
                                            CIP

Printed and bound in the United States of America.
10 9 8 7 6 5 4 3

Acknowledgements

I would like to thank my mother, Darlene Eborg, and my father, Don Wilber, who have contributed significantly to the text of this book.

Thank you to my sisters, Lisa and Denise, my brother, Ken and his wife Wendy, each of whom helped with the writing, typing, and moral support.

Thank you to my assistant Robert Anderson, who was a big help with the researching and editing of the manuscript.

And most of all, thank you to the readers, who have shown the interest to take their own problems to court. Good Luck!

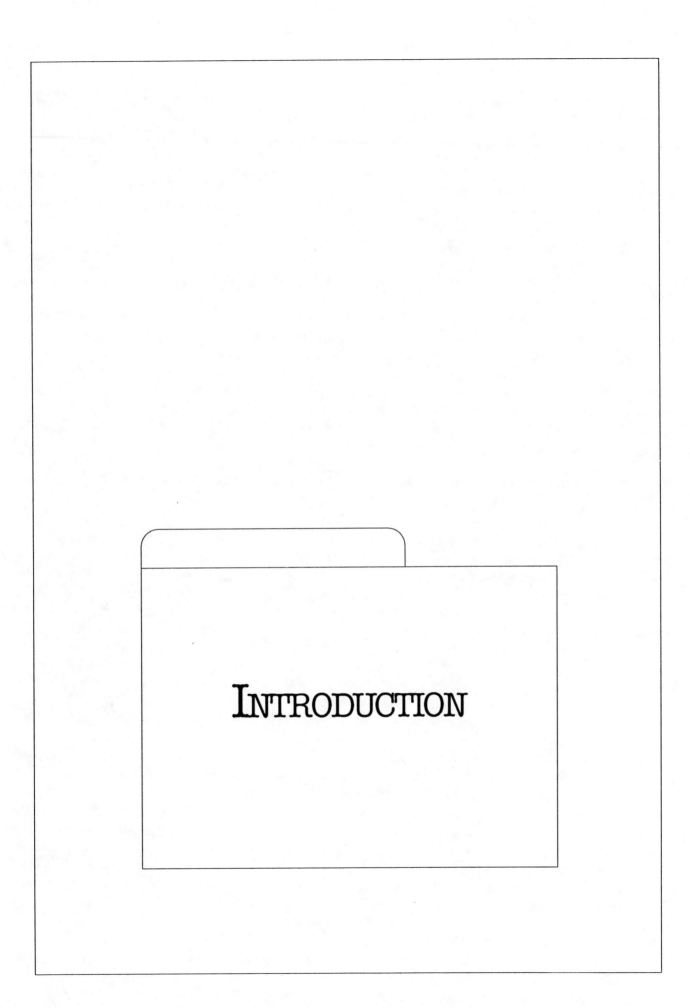

INTRODUCTION

If you are a creditor with a debt collection problem, someone is playing games with your money. If you want it all back, with interest and costs, you have to play the game too. The game with real people, real issues and real money, has rules like any other game. This book explains the rules in your court and the strategy to play the game. It's the only game in town where the odds and justice are on your side. Although a victory cannot be guaranteed, this book will give you guidance into the avenues open to you, enabling you to find your way through the small claims court system as a confident individual, without the professional services of a lawyer.

The situations that arise in small claims court vary greatly; however, by definition, small claims only handles small civil matters. That is, noncriminal matters with claims involving only a few thousand dollars.

The following types of cases are typical of a small claims court docket:

1. Landlord-tenant problems. Either the landlord suing for rent or eviction or the tenant suing to get the deposit back.

2. Contract actions involving labor performed. This may involve a painter who painted a house and a homeowner who refuses to pay the bill.

3. Contract actions involving an unpaid bill. This may be a hospital suing to recover the money owed by a patient. It may involve a small business owner suing to recover goods sold on credit.

4. Tort (Injurious) actions. This may involve an automobile accident where the driver would like to be compensated for damage to the vehicle or damage to his or her own body.

These are only a few types of cases that you will see in a small claims court on any typical day. By taking your claim to small claims court, you are taking advantage of a convenient and economical way of solving your collection problem.

Do You Have a Case?

Things to Consider Before Filing a Lawsuit

1. Do you have the time it takes to go to court? (i.e. will your boss or your business allow you to take a couple of hours off for the hearing?)

2. Do you have the money up front that it takes to file the lawsuit and serve the defendant?

   Filing fees are listed in Chapter 7 for each individual state. Service of summons on the defendant runs typically from $12.00 to $30.00, depending on the state.

3. Were you wronged (damaged) in some way? To file a lawsuit, you must have been wronged in some way. Typically, in small claims court the wrong will either fit under the category of a contract action or a negligence action. A contract action includes such items as: 1) you perform a service of some type (painted defendant's house), 2) defendant has failed to pay on his account (purchasing tools at the hardware store on credit), 3) defendant signed a contract stating he would pay you money at a certain time (a contract to purchase a car).

   A negligence action in small claims court typically deals with personal or property damage sustained. A perfect example is an automobile accident where defendant is at fault. You bring an action in small claims court to make him pay for your broken toe (personal damage) and the dents in the side of your car (property damage).

4. Can you put the damage in monetary terms? The court must have a specific dollar figure from you. To compute the amount, see Chapter 2.

5. Are you suing the correct party? You don't want to waste your time in court. Make sure you know who the correct

party is to be sued before filing the lawsuit.

6. Is the defendant still in the state? It is often very difficult to serve a defendant who has moved out of the state. It is also very difficult to collect once a judgement is received. Suing a defendant and collecting on the judgement from an out of state defendant goes outside the realm of this book. Additional research would have to be done at a local law library to determine what your state allows and the methods to accomplish the task.

7. Can the defendant be easily found? The harder he is to find, the higher the fee will be to serve him. If the sheriff cannot serve him, you may have to hire a private process server or private investigator. For the tough cases, this service is expensive.

8. Will you be able to collect the money once you have a judgement? As the saying goes, you can't get blood out of a turnip. A judgement isn't worth the paper it's printed on if the debtor-defendant has no money, no job, no assets, and no desire to pay you.

With attorneys and collection agencies making a nice living from plaintiffs like you, it is only logical that once you know the game rules, you can save money too.

Chapter 1

EFFECTIVE
IN-HOUSE
COLLECTION
TECHNIQUES

Although this book is titled *Small Claims Court Without a Lawyer*, it is also important to emphasize that many debts can be settled prior to legal action. Several different techniques can be utilized in the collection of a debt.

Written correspondence and telephone techniques are instrumental in successfully satisfying a debt. The suggested pattern in this book is the use of written correspondence as the initial method of debt collection. If this method does not achieve the desired results, telephone collection techniques are clearly outlined. Through this method, you can use your powers of persuasion to achieve great results. If these initial methods prove unsuccessful, you may wish to try a last ditch effort with a final demand letter. If all efforts fail, it is time to go to court. Samples of the collection letters described below are included in Appendix A.

Collection Letters

First Demand Letter

All letters sent should be tactfully written. You do not want to alienate the other party; you want to resolve the problem. If you own a business, your letter may gently remind a forgetful debtor of a bill. If you are an individual with a complaint against a company, be sure to send the letter to the individual at the company who has the authority to do something about your problem.

Payment Plan Letter

For some debtors, a payment plan is the only way in which they will ever satisfy a bill. A letter that stipulates the terms of the oral agreement is a handy way to keep everyone up to date.

Delinquent Payments Letter

At some point, the debtor may need to be reminded about a payment plan on which he or she has fallen behind. Be firm and demand that the debtor catch up immediately. Explain that the ramifications of not dealing with the problem will be legal action initiated by you.

Settlement Letter

Sometimes it is best to cut your losses and agree on a settlement figure. Some debtors will jump at the chance to settle for less than the full amount. Whether you choose to settle or not depends on the strength of your case, and the amount of time and money you are willing to spend to fight for the extra percentage.

Final Demand Letter

A final demand letter should be used as a last-ditch effort to demand payment from the debtor. It warns the debtor in a practical and matter-of-fact way of the consequences of not paying the bill and not responding to previous letters. It should be worded in a way which creates a sense of urgency in resolving the matter.

The letter should be sent by certified mail, return receipt requested. It is important to stress the seriousness of this matter in every way.

Telephone Strategies

Most businesses would prefer to settle accounts instead of filing suit against their clients. Most individuals would also prefer to settle their disputes instead of filing suit. One method for lowering the percentages of cases that go to court is to incorporate the collection phone call. It is amazing the results a phone call can have on some people. It is often embarrassing to receive such a call. Many debtors will immediately promise to get the money to you or your business. If you own a business, you may discover that the debtor has a dispute with your company over products or services furnished. If this can be resolved amicably, it may result in yet another satisfied customer rather than a disgruntled one who refuses to pay a bill. If you are an individual, you may discover that the debtor-company is quite willing to work with you in resolving the dispute so as to save a valued customer.

A creditor such as yourself must be careful in the manner that phone calls are made. Phone calls should be reasonable and businesslike and should not be made in a harassing, misrepresentative, or abusive manner.

Telephone collection requires planning and preparation. The following steps should be thought through before the call and followed during the conversation.

Be Organized

Gather all bills and other information about the claim for quick reference. Review all information immediately before the call.

Identify Yourself

If you are calling on behalf of a business, state your name, title and the business you represent. If you are an individual with a claim against a company, state your name and reason for calling.

Speak to the Correct Person

To get prompt action, you must speak directly to the debtor or the person in charge of handling the claim at the debtor-company. *Note: Some states even impose liability for disclosing information to the wrong person.*

Introductory Phone Comments

Clearly identify the claim you are speaking of and state the exact amount owed, when the debt was incurred and the fact that the debtor has had adequate time to make payment.

If you are an individual with a claim against a company, give your account number and briefly, in a few sentences, explain the situation.

Strategies of Asking for Payment (business v. debtor)

Always begin with payment in full only. At this point do not give any indication that you may accept an installment payment plan. Your goal is to receive a check for the entire amount on the following business day. Do not lose sight of the goal. Insist that immediate payment of your debt is more important than payment of any other possible debts. This debt was incurred some time ago and has become quite delinquent and you refuse to accept further excuses.

In the alternative, set up installment payments. When you give up the idea of payment in full, suggest installment payments of a large amount. Begin with at least one-half of the debt and negotiate from there. Remember, you may have to remind the debtor of each installment, so do not agree to small payments that will cause you periodic headaches.

You may wish to send a letter confirming the payment plan. A form letter is found in Appendix A.

Strategies of Asking for Satisfaction (individual v. business)

Upon reaching the party in charge of making decisions for the business and briefly explaining the problem, tactfully request that they resolve the problem, i.e., to fix the roof or supply a new product. If you talk to someone high enough up in the company, it is often surprising the results you may see. If you do not achieve results at this level, you may wish to send a final demand letter to the president or owner of the company with a deadline for action. Stick by this deadline. If they do not respond satisfactorily, it is time to take legal action.

Settlements and How to Make Them Sound Appealing

There are cost savings on both sides when a disputed or uncollected debt is settled. The creditor saves the time and expense of litigation, while the debtor saves his credit rating and does not have to pay wage garnishments and other court costs. Make these advantages clear to the debtor.

Upon agreement of a settlement figure, send written confirmation of this amount to the debtor. A form settlement letter is found in Appendix A.

Tactics to Avoid Using

Do not threaten. There is no reason to do so. The law has given you the avenue of the small claims court to avoid such action.

Do not state actions that you cannot or do not plan to carry out. You can tell them what to expect in terms of your further actions and you plan on taking this to court if they do not pay. You can also tell them the assets you can attach if they do not pay the judgment. (See Chapter 7.)

Closing Statements

Always leave the conversation on a firm note. The debtor should know that you plan to be reasonable, yet firm in your demands. Give them a deadline. Make it clear that if they do not respond on that day, you will immediately take further action. This may entail legal action or some sort of agency action. If you are dealing with a business, you may indicate that an agency such as the Better Business Bureau will be notified if they fail to cooperate.

Most Frequently Used Excuses and How to Counter

The check is in the mail.

We have all heard this excuse a thousand times. If this is your first phone contact with the debtor, give him the benefit of the doubt. Tell the person that you will give the check two or three days to get to you. If it is not there within that time, take immediate further action.

I am unemployed.

In times of recession this will be a common excuse. You will need to work closely with unemployed individuals. Suggest an installment payment plan. This can coincide with their unemployment check or other periodic incoming money.

**My ex-husband was supposed to pay that bill,
it said so in the divorce decree.**

You as a creditor were not a party to the divorce decree. Therefore, you are not bound by it. If both parties were obliged to pay you the money, both parties are still so obliged.

For example, you loan $200 to husband and wife. The husband and wife subsequently get a divorce. In the divorce decree, the husband is required to pay you the $200, but does not follow through. You then sue them both in small claims court and get a judgment against both. The wife is the only one that has any money and so you garnish her wages or her bank account until the debt is paid. If she then chooses to take her ex-husband back to court to be reimbursed, that is up to her.

Other excuses:

I have too many expenses to pay you too.

I don't have the money.

I just had a baby.

Stress the importance of paying the bill. Emphasize that the bill is quite overdue and that you plan on carrying through with the process until the bill is paid. The debtor can either work with you now and pay just the bill itself or ignore the warnings and be forced to pay judgment interest and court costs in addition.

You may also request that they send you a statement of their current finances. Request that they fill out the Affidavit of Assets and Liabilities (see Appendix A). This will give you an indication of where they stand financially. If you have access, you may wish to run a credit check on the individual for an accurate survey of the situation.

Chapter 2

FILING AND SERVING THE LAWSUIT

Small Claims Court

Overview

Small claims cases must comply with each individual state's civil procedure laws, just as must all larger civil cases. Small claims court, because it was designed for the layman, has relaxed rules of evidence and procedure. Small claims court handles only civil matters. For example, an action for money damages or wrongful, injurious conduct. It does not handle any criminal matters. It is in the small claims arena the average person can file a claim and get a judgment, quickly and economically, typically without an attorney's assistance.

You can count on making at least two trips to the courthouse—the first to file the claim and the second for the hearing. You will file your claim with the clerk's office. The monetary limitation in small claims court varies from state-to-state, as set by the state legislature. (See Chapter 7 for each state's limit.) Larger amounts which do not fit within this limit are filed in different divisions of the clerk's office, under different headings with larger filing fees. It is within these larger arenas that it is advisable to hire an attorney to lend legal guidance. It is also within these larger arenas that the stricter rules of evidence apply. The parties must be well versed in examining and cross examining witnesses, giving opening and closing remarks, objecting to errors in the opposing party's statements and form of questioning, as well as a multitude of other topics.

The object of small claims court is to take the burden of strict evidentiary rules away and allow the layman to litigate his or her claim in an environment that is not as threatening as is the larger civil arena.

Venue

The claim or complaint must typically be filed in either the county where the facts gave rise to the cause of action or the county in which the defendant is a resident. Some states only allow the claim to be filed where the defendant is a resident.

Statutes of Limitation

One possibly fatal error is to sit on a case until the statute of limitations has run out. This means that the claim was not filed with the clerk's office within the time limits set by the state legislature. It is important to check with your individual state's laws as to the time limits (see Chapter 7 for your state's limitations). The time stops ticking on the day the claim is filed with the clerk, not on the day it is heard by the court.

If the action is not filed within the designated time, it will more than likely be thrown out at the time of filing by the clerk or thrown out by the judge at the first hearing.

To compute the time remaining on your action, look to see when the act was done or the contract was signed. On an account where the defendant did not make a scheduled payment, figure from the time the payment was due.

Examples of this action include tenants moving out of an apartment, leaving three months left on a signed lease. The action begins at the time the tenant neglects to pay the monthly rent. From this point on, the plaintiff landlord has only a specified number of years in which to file the action for money damages against the tenants.

Another example is an electrician who provides electrical work to a customer who later refuses to pay for the work. The electrician has a specific number of years, depending on the state, in which to file an action from the date the customer first owed the money.

Depending on the state, in tort cases, time is often computed from the time of the injury or the time the plaintiff first knew of the injury.

The Clerk's Office

The courthouse can be an intimidating place for a newcomer. The clerk's office is often large and very busy. Because of the large volume of work they handle, clerks can be impatient, expecting one to know the procedure for filing cases, the costs involved, and where to go for forms and documents. Don't be alarmed or distraught, a friendly word and a smile often slows their pace enough to give you the additional attention you require. The clerk's office has a monstrous volume of work to handle and it is up to you to persevere in your endeavors.

The clerks will often be able to give only limited advice. They are not attorneys and are not allowed to practice law, but can give you general guidance in proceeding with your case.

Some clerks' offices have specific forms used in their courts, these are the only forms they will accept. Other clerks don't seem to mind how or on what the complaint is written. A clerk once told me that she didn't mind if the complaint came in on toilet paper. As you can see, as local governments and local rules vary, so will the procedures of each individual court. Fortunately, many court systems provide helpful explanatory booklets on using the local system. Inquire with the small claims clerk in your county for the local rules and procedures.

Appendix A includes forms used in small claims court. These are only examples. It will be necessary for you to obtain the specific forms from the local clerk for the county in which you are filing suit. However, from the forms included in this book, you will be able to determine the information necessary to complete local forms.

Filing the Lawsuit

The document that is necessary completed to initiate the proceedings is typically referred to as the Complaint, Statement of Claim, or Petition. (See Appendix A) It is the document on which you list your name or business, the defendant's name or business, the amount owed and the reason for the debt. Each small claims clerk's office will have the form necessary for their specific county. How detailed you need to be in stating your claim varies from courthouse to courthouse. A majority of the explanation will be done in front of the judge, so many judges require very little explanation on the complaint.

There will be a fee for filing the complaint. This amount varies; however, it is usually a fairly reasonable sum, and far less than the filing fee for larger-dollar lawsuits (outside small claims court dollar limits).

Computing the Amount of Your Claim

Items Which Typically Can Be Included:

1. The amount of the service performed, the debt accrued, the property damage sustained, or the amount contracted for, depending on the type of case.

2. If there was a signed contract which stated such; attorney's fees, prejudgement interest, and any damages listed.

3. Subpoena fees for witnesses, if necessary.

4. The cost of the filing fee and the service of the summons.

Items Which Typically Cannot Be Included:

1. The value of your time in collecting the debt and going to the courthouse, i.e. lost wages from work and gas spent getting to the courthouse.

2. Your attorney's fees if defendant did not sign a contract agreeing to such or the state statute does not allow.

Service of Process on an Individual

Before a claim may be brought before a judge, the defendant must be served with the complaint (also called a statement of claim or petition). Typically, once the complaint is filed with the clerk's office, the clerk will give the claim a case number. The original copy must then be served on the defendant.

The summons (also called the notice) is the document that is attached to the complaint and gives instructions on who must be served. There are three basic methods of serving a summons. The first is service by the U.S. Mail. The second is service by a sheriff or deputy. The third is service by a private process server. Each of these three will be discussed below in greater detail. Be aware that different counties and different states allow various methods of one or more of these types of service. (See Chapter 7 for the methods acceptable in your state.)

U.S. Mail

Some states and counties allow for the service of summons through the mail. The requirement that it be certified, return receipt requested, is often a further stipulation.

There are various benefits of using this form of service. Time and expense are saved in avoiding hiring a person to serve the papers. The defendant is also saved the embarrassment of being served legal papers at work or home.

The detriments include the fact that receiving a summons through the mail is not as effective in grabbing the defendant's attention. The experienced debtor will be aware of the contents of the letter he is to sign for and will refuse to sign for it at the post office. If he doesn't sign, it isn't a valid service. At this juncture, a more expensive alternative must be chosen.

Sheriff

The thought of a sheriff coming to the door has a very serious effect on most people. Dressed in that official uniform and delivering court documents, the officer is an effective method of impressing upon a defendant that this is a serious matter requiring immediate attention.

In addition, you may instruct the sheriff to serve the defendant at his or her place of employment. Some sheriffs' offices allow this practice, others do not. It is often a highly embarrassing situation to be served at work in front of colleagues. This is a strategy for you to consider in your pre-trial plans.

Depending on the county, the sheriff will either serve the person and bill you for services or will request a fee in advance (often the actual cost of service plus mileage) before attempting service.

The sheriff does a good job; however, a lot of services must be completed each day. The sheriff cannot spend the entire day on your particular matter. If a defendant cannot be found by the second or third try, the sheriff often sends the summons and complaint back with a bill for the attempted service.

At this point, you may need to do a little investigation on your own to determine the location of the party and the best time and place to serve him or her. If your investigation is not fruitful and the case is important enough, a private investigator should be retained.

Upon locating the party, an alias summons can be obtained from the clerk's office at a minimal charge. This summons looks just like the original summons, but has the word "Alias" typed in front of the title, "Summons". You may wish to add any additional information you have found regarding best time and place for service onto the summons directly, or attached to it on a document called a Praecipe. (See Appendix A.)

If you do not wish to go through the sheriff's office again, the private process server is a viable alternative which has become quite popular over the last few years.

Private Process Service

Most states will allow any person to be a private process server, as long as that person is not a party to the case, is at least 18 years old and there has been a motion filed and an order signed by the judge allowing such service (see Chapter 7).

The advantages of using private process servers can include:

1. Cost—they are often inexpensive, so as to be competitive with the sheriff's office.

2. Quickness—they often can serve within hours if requested.

3. Flexibility—many will serve anywhere, anytime so as to effectively serve the party in question.

The disadvantages can include:

1. Unless the private process server is a licensed detective or working under one, a Motion for Private Process Service and an Order for Private Process Service typically will have to be filed with each case.

2. You must find a reputable process server. You don't want to get burned by an unethical individual or company. The clerk's office will often know of one or two highly rated private process servers who practice extensively throughout the county.

Inquire with the clerk of the court whether you will need a motion and an order from the judge to use a private process server. If so, ask if there is a specific form the clerk would prefer you use. If not, use the Motion and Order for Private Process Service Form in Appendix A as a guide in preparing your documents.

Be aware that the court will automatically dismiss your case if the defendant is not served within the required time limits. Nebraska's limitation, for example, is six months from the time of filing the action. If the defendant is not served within the time frame, the case will most likely be dismissed without prejudice. This means that you are allowed to re-file the claim, pay the filing fee and attempt to re-serve the defendant.

Service of Process on a Business

The method for filing and serving a business will probably be different from the way a case is filed and served against an individual.

Sole Proprietorship

A sole proprietorship is a business owned by an individual who remains personally liable for all debts incurred by the business. Typically, the way you list the defendant in the complaint and summons is to list the individual's name followed by the name he or she is doing business as, e.g., Tom Egert, d/b/a Longbranch Vintage Clothing. The defendant is then served as an individual, as described in the text above. Once you get a judgment, you can go after both Tom Egert and his business, Longbranch Vintage Clothing, to satisfy the debt.

Partnership

A partnership can come in various forms, with general partners and limited partners. General partners are personally liable for debts of the business. Limited partners are liable only to the extent they have invested in the business. Once again, the way to list a partnership on a complaint may vary from state-to-state. However, generally you must list each general partner, noting he or she as such, followed by the name in which the person is doing business as, e.g., Kenneth Lee, a general partner, and Wendy Kline, a general partner, d/b/a R.T.W. Express Co. Once you get a judgment, you may proceed against any or all general partners and/or the business to collect the judgment.

Corporation

A corporation is treated as an entity separate from its stockholders and officers (owners). The owners are not personally responsible for the debts of the business. Therefore, the corporation itself is sued. Although, typically the registered agent is the person to be served, this varies from state-to-state (see Chapter 7). You must list the correct corporate name on the court documents. This information can be obtained through your state's secretary of state office. For example, you want to sue Soundcore Music because the equipment purchased didn't work correctly. Upon calling your particular state's secretary of state, you find that the registered agent must be served to get effective service of process. You also find that Soundcore Music's officially filed name is Joe C's Soundcore Music Headquarters for Great Tunes, Inc. On the complaint, the corporate defendant's name must read exactly as it is officially filed.

A judgment obtained against a corporation can be enforced only against the business. If an individual in a corporation personally wronged you, you may be able to sue that person individually. An example of this is the corporation B & K's Shooters' and Accessories, a business which reloads shotgun shells. An employee, Mr. Major, reloads a shell incorrectly and it is sent off to the customer. The customer shoots the shell and is seriously injured. The customer can then sue the corporation, as well as the individual who was responsible for the damage (Mr. Major). However, the customer may not sue the owners of the corporation. They will typically not be responsible, since they are legally protected from personal liability by the corporation.

Changing a Court Date

If the date set for your hearing becomes impossible to attend or you are not prepared, you will need to change the date. This can be done in three ways.

The first is to get the opposing party to consent to the date change. Have a few dates in mind when calling the party. Ask him if he would mind if the hearing date was changed and give him some dates from which to pick. Upon the defendant consenting, call the clerk and let her know. She may require the two parties to complete some type of consent form.

The second is to file a motion for continuance with the court. Each clerk's forms are different, so contact the clerk for a copy of the form you need. Along with the motion, there will be an order which the judge will sign if he grants your motion. A copy of this order should go both to you and the defendant.

The third is to appear before the judge on the day of the hearing and explain why you are not ready to litigate the case, asking for a continuance at that time. This is the riskiest method, however. The judge may or may not grant your request. If he denies your request, you are stuck litigating the matter that day, even if not prepared.

Typically, most judges will grant each party at least one continuance. So, use your privilege wisely, and if you must get a continuance, try the methods in the order listed.

Chapter 3

THE TRIAL

Preliminary Hearings

The first court date is called the hearing. In some states, only the defendant is required to appear at this time. In other states, both parties must appear. The latter is the scenario that will be discussed here.

It is often at the hearing that Plaintiff and Defendant meet face-to-face for the first time. It is often an awkward time, especially without the assistance of attorneys. The parties should get together and attempt to resolve the conflict before this point if possible. If no compromise can be reached, go ahead and take a seat in the courtroom. The courtroom is often crowded with other individuals suing or being sued. In states where attorneys are allowed in small claims court, quite a few attorneys will be present for their clients.

The typical procedure for most courthouses is that small claims preliminary hearings are all set for one particular day and time each week. The bailiff should have a listing of the cases set for that date and whether there was service on the defendant(s).

When the judge enters the courtroom, it is usually the procedure for all present to rise. When once again seated, the clerk or the judge will begin calling the cases. Watch what other parties do in their cases, so that you know what to do, where to stand, when to speak. When it is your turn to be heard, approach the bench and politely respond only when asked a question. You want to be sure to avoid alienating the judge. Although judges are supposed to be impartial, they are human and you risk swaying them against your side.

Often if the parties have failed to attempt to negotiate first, the judge may request the parties to step into a side room and discuss their problem. It is at this time that you need to remain calm, cool, and collected. Speak to the other party in a courteous, but matter-of-fact manner. Explain your viewpoint in an organized way and listen while the other party speaks. If you are willing to negotiate, ask the other party if he or she is willing to settle.

If the answer is yes, suggest an amount with which you feel comfortable, while still giving yourself some negotiating room. If the problem can be solved before having the court settle the matter, typically all parties are more pleased with the outcome.

Default Hearings

If you show up, the other party does not and was properly served, the judge will probably enter a Default Judgment in your favor. This means that the other party has defaulted its position by not appearing.

The other party may petition the court within a reasonable time to get the Default Judgment set aside if they have a good reason (the timetable differs slightly from state-to-state).

However, if the allotted time comes and goes and you have heard nothing, the judgment is deemed permanent.

At this point a post judgment letter needs to be written to the defendant. This letter should announce that you have received a judgment and are now expecting it to be paid. It may also warn the debtor of further action you intend on taking to collect the money. (See Appendix A.)

Be careful, just as the judge will enter judgment in your favor, if the defendant does not appear at the required time, so he may enter judgment in defendant's favor or dismiss your case if you do not appear at the required time. If neither party appears, the judge will likely dismiss the action. Usually this dismissal is without prejudice, meaning you may refile the case with the clerk, re-pay the filing fee, and proceed through the steps again.

Contested Hearings

If both you and the opposing party show up at the preliminary hearing and are ready to litigate the claim, the judge may do one of two things. The judge may hear the case that day or may "set it over for trial" to another day. It often depends on the state laws, the particular judge's style and how crowded the courtroom is that particular day.

If it is within the state law and the judge's style to have the case heard that very hour, you must be prepared with your witnesses and evidence. Whether the judge operates in this fashion can be discovered from either the clerk's office or the judge's secretary. If you can't get this information in advance, it is better to be safe than sorry. Bring your witnesses and evidence to the first hearing.

If the judge sets the case over for trial, take advantage of the additional time. Attempt settlement negotiations if feasible, plan trial strategies, go over your evidence and the testimony of your witnesses. Wear a nice dress or suit—a conservative, professional appearance never hurts.

The judge may have a variety of different ways of conducting a small claims trial. Each party may be invited to stand in front of the bench to speak his or her mind. The judge may then ask a few questions and make a decision on the spot. If the issues are complex, the parties may be asked to have a seat at the respective plaintiff and defendant tables and begin hearing the case in a more formal style.

During the more formal trial, the plaintiff will have a chance to speak, call witnesses, and introduce evidence first. The defendant has the right to cross examine each witness that the plaintiff puts on the stand. Once the plaintiff's evidence is presented, it is the defendant's turn to speak, call witnesses, and introduce evidence. The plaintiff also has the right to cross examine each witness the defendant puts on the stand. Once this is complete, the plaintiff has the right to a final statement concerning the case. At this point, the judge may give a decision or take the matter under advisement and mail a decision to the parties.

Some situations do require an attorney's expertise. This may be where the opposing side files affirmative defenses, files a counter-claim, or hires an attorney. You must weigh the odds and see which way is best for your situation.

If your income is below a minimum amount, a legal clinic can give you guidance. College students may seek assistance from the campus legal aid office. If you are a senior citizen or handicapped, many law schools offer a free legal clinic. There may also be a free legal hotline or information number in your state. See Chapter 7 for information concerning your individual state. The bar association in your state may also be able to give you information on where to turn (see Appendix B).

Chapter 4

Post-Judgment

In many instances, the defendant, now commonly referred to as the judgment debtor, is not going to voluntarily pay the judgment. Every state allows you to take recourse. This recourse, referred to as "executing on the judgment," varies greatly from state-to-state.

This chapter will give you a general overall picture of the process. The types of execution allowed by your state are listed in Chapter 7.

Sample forms necessary are shown in Appendix A. Please note that certain clerk's offices are often very particular concerning the form used in their court, and they may request that you use the forms provided by their office.

Execution on the judgment is your responsibility, not the court's. You must handle this matter in a timely fashion. The act of executing on the judgment is limited to the life of the judgment. This lifetime varies from state-to-state.

Execution on the judgment is typically not allowed until after a final judgment is received in a case. It may not be allowed until the judgment is recorded with the clerk's office. It also may not be allowed until after the time has run in which the defendant could file a motion for a new trial or rehearing.

Listed below are the various methods used by plaintiffs in recovering moneys owed. Your situation and the state you live in will determine the method best chosen for your case.

Garnishments (for wages, bank accounts, and independent contractors)

If the defendant is not willing to sit down and write out a check in your name, most states have provided methods of collection through garnishment. States vary widely on their strictness and methods of garnishment. For instance, the leeway given to plaintiffs with the use of Wage Garnishments and Non-Wage Garnishments in Illinois is a luxury that plaintiffs in all states do not have. For example, Florida and Texas are very debtor-oriented. It is very difficult to garnish wages, bank accounts, and real property from many debtors who are low income and/or a head of a household. Florida and Texas have very strict homestead exemption and head-of-household laws. Most other states fit somewhere in between these two extremes. The circuit clerk will know the rules on which collection methods are allowable in your state and county. The clerk will most likely have the specific forms that the court prefers the plaintiffs to use. Be sure to ask.

Wage Garnishments

The information needed for a wage garnishment are included on the Affidavit for Wage Deduction Order and the Wage Deduction Summons in Appendix A. These documents must be filed at the clerk's office, typically along with a minimal filing fee. Some clerks prepare the documents themselves. If so, this is one less job for you. One phone call to the clerk will let you know whether you must use the forms on hand in their office and if you must prepare the documents. The clerk will then collect the filing fee, sign the documents, and give them to the applicable person to have the service made on the debtor's employer. States' instructions to an employer vary, but the following are typical.

An employer is required to withhold the following from a non-exempt employee's salary: the lesser of 1.) 25% per week of the gross amount paid the employee for any work week or 2.) the amount by which disposable earnings of said employee for a week exceed thirty times the federal minimum hourly wage in effect at the time the amounts are payable. The term "disposable earnings" means that part of the earnings of any individual remaining after the deduction from those earnings of any amounts required by law to be withheld.

Some states allow for a continuing writ of garnishment, which allows the employer to continue garnishing the debtor's wages week after week until the debt is satisfied. Your state's law is listed in Chapter 7.

As in the example above, the garnishment continues in effect for a specific amount of weeks or until the debt is paid, depending on the specific state. At the completion of the stated time, the employer will send you and the court a copy of the interrogatories he or she has filled out. The employer may send the check to you directly, send it to the clerk, or may hold it and request an order from the judge to release the funds.

Different employers have different habits. Different courts have different rules. After the judgment is obtained, you can find out the habit of the particular employer by calling the payroll department of the garnished company and asking for the person in charge of wage garnishments.

If the full amount of the judgment is not garnished within the time allowed, another Wage Garnishment will be necessary. Retype the Affidavit for Wage Deduction Order to reflect the amount paid by the employer and the amount remaining due. Refile this with the circuit clerk's office. There may be another fee for filing. Fortunately, these fees can typically be billed to the defendant.

Non-Wage Garnishments (Bank Accounts)

If you know the debtor has a bank account with a satisfactory sum of money in it, a Non-Wage Garnishment is often a very quick and effective way of receiving payment for the debt.

The first step is to file the necessary documents with the clerk. It will then need to be served upon the bank holding the funds. The Non-Wage Deduction Order and Summons instructs the bank to put a hold on any funds currently in the debtor's name (see Appendix A).

Independent Contractor

If your debtor is an independent contractor with money owed to him by his employer, the non-wage garnishment is the avenue to use. The garnishment is served upon the employer and any monies owed to the defendant are held and monies up to the amount of the judgment are then turned over to you. The employer often will request an order signed by the judge allowing him to release the funds. This is used by the employer to avoid the liability of turning the money over to the wrong person.

Depositions, Citations to Discover Assets, Interrogatories

If you are not aware of what or where assets of the defendant may be located, a deposition (also called a Citation to Discover Assets or Interrogatories), is the legal avenue in which to proceed (see Appendix A). The subpoena is a document requiring the debtor to appear either in court or at your place of business (depending on the state) to produce all books, papers, or records in his or her possession or control that may contain information concerning the property or income of, or indebtedness due you. If you know of any special documents that may show where the debtor has wealth, you should name these in the document as well. Often what you will be looking for includes place of employment, real estate, personal property, such as vehicles and boats, bank accounts, and stocks and bonds.

At the hearing, take along a form for the defendant to fill out (see Appendix A). Once you are armed with this completed form, you are ready to garnish wages and bank accounts, attach property, and collect on other items the defendant may have.

If it does not appear that the defendant has any assets, you may be stuck for the time being. However, judgments are valid for quite a few years, (see Chapter 7 for the length of time in your state) and you are allowed by the court to repeat this deposition again in the future.

Rule to Show Cause (Contempt of Court)

If the debtor does not appear for the Deposition or Citation to Discover Assets, a Rule to Show Cause (also called a Motion for Contempt) may be served upon the debtor. This is a document which orders the debtor to appear before the judge and explain why he or she was not at the deposition (Citation to Discover Assets hearing). It is often at this hearing that the judge will then order the debtor to talk to you about available assets. Upon completion, the judge may then ask both parties to step forward and inquire as to whether the debtor has been candid about financial information and whether a payment arrangement has been agreed upon.

Bench Warrants

If the defendant-debtor does not appear for any of the hearings up to this point, depending on the state, a bench warrant may be issued for his or her arrest. This is often a fast way of getting a debtor's attention. Jail can have a truly sobering effect. It opens many peoples' eyes to the seriousness of the matter. A bond will be set by the judge. The debtor will have to pay this bond to get out of jail. As a result, you are often quickly paid.

Remember, even though debtors can't go to jail because they are poor, they can go to jail if they ignore court orders.

Attachment, Levy, or Execution on Personal Property

Depending on the individual and the state, the court may allow some taking of a debtor's personal property. However, this is often a very difficult task. If you know of property that the debtor owns which is not subject to other liens and is not exempt personal property under state law, you may request a Writ of Attachment from the clerk's office. There may be a fee for this service. This document contains a listing of the assets that are to be picked up by the sheriff. The writ is given to the sheriff who will proceed to follow its directions. A fee is paid, either to the clerk or the sheriff, along with a bond to protect the debtor in case the assets were taken wrongfully. This is typically a substantial amount of money.

Automobiles

You must be specific in the assets you are requesting. If it is an automobile, you must list the model, color, tag number, vehicle identification number, approximate value of the vehicle, whether it is subject to any other liens, and location of the vehicle on the writ. You can get information on a vehicle by calling the state's Department of Motor Vehicles.

Once the automobile has been seized, it will be held by the sheriff's department to be sold at a sheriff's auction. Often the debtor will contact you before the vehicle is sold. This is a good time to negotiate the debt. Often, if the debtor will pay the debt and all court costs, a satisfaction of judgment can be filed, the sale can be stopped, and the vehicle returned to the defendant.

Caution! Be sure that the debtor has quite a bit of equity in the vehicle. If the debtor just recently purchased the car and is paying monthly on it to a bank, that bank is going to get the first monies from the sale to pay off the debt owed them. Make sure that you are making it worth your while and your money to attach it.

Business Property

If you have received a judgment against a business, it is often possible to attach assets of the business. This can include business machinery, cash register receipts, and office equipment. To establish the assets the business has and when the most money is in the cash register, you may wish to do a deposition on the company first. This way you will be fully knowledgeable and prepared when you complete the Writ of Attachment for the sheriff.

Other Personal Possessions

Furniture, boats, airplanes, jewelry, stock, and many other items may be attachable. Once again, a detailed explanation of the item is necessary for the sheriff's Writ of Attachment. If the item is a boat or airplane, you will need information similar to that described above regarding automobiles. You will also need to know the approximate value of the goods, whether they are subject to any other liens, and their location.

Liens on Real Property

The threat of placing a lien on a debtor's property may well be incentive enough to persuade him or her to pay the judgment. A lien on real property is a legal claim to property. A piece of property can have more than one lien. Each will have a different priority of claim.

In some states a lien is placed on a defendant's property automatically when a judgment is entered against him or her (see Chapter 7).

A copy of the judgment needs to be filed in each county in which the defendant has real property. The form, referred to as an Abstract of Judgment or a similar name, can be found at the clerk's office. Proper filing will give you a valid lien and add your name to the list of lienholders on the property.

The simple act of placing a lien on the property does not force a sale of the property. It only places a claim against the property, if and when it is sold. When it is sold, the order of the liens on the property will determine the order in which profits will be divided.

Homestead laws in most states exempt part or all of a debtor's home from attachment or levy. In most states a lien can be put on the property; however, a creditor such as yourself may not force a sale of the property. This protection typically lasts though the life of the debtor, sometimes through the life of the spouse. The protection also lasts only as long as the debtor occupies the house and claims it to be homestead. If the debtor were to move and rent out the house, it would no longer be considered homestead and would become levyable.

Chapter 5

PREVENTIVE MEASURES

Get It in Writing

If your dispute involved the defendant's word against yours, you have probably already learned a valuable lesson. Get everything in writing! When it comes to proving your case in front of a judge, it is far easier to point to a document with the defendant's signature rather than to try to reiterate the earlier agreement.

In the future, use a written rather than oral contract. For other problems, make notes of what happened as soon as possible after it happens. The following paragraphs highlight some quick tips on when written documents can help you, and why.

Written Contracts

As just noted, written contracts, when signed by both parties, help eliminate most disputes. Also, it wouldn't hurt to get witnesses to also sign the contract, and even to get it notarized. The notarization proves that the other party signed the paper, and, when reminded that the contract was notarized, it might make the other party feel guilty in the eyes of the law about having broken the deal. Having witnesses sign proves that the they were present when the deal was made, and their memories can help clear up points of dispute as to what was agreed. Of course, if the witnesses are on your side, this helps more.

Written Notes

Writing down your impression of what just happened helps create a record for the court, and it also will help you keep track of the sequence of events. For example, if someone works on your car, and you feel it wasn't fixed correctly, you might take it back to the garage two, maybe three, maybe more, times. Each of these times it would be helpful to keep track of what the symptoms were and what the mechanic said he or she "fixed" each time.

IOU's

In the case of loans or rental agreements—even when you loan someone a book or lawn mower—if you get it in writing, the paper will help remind you and, most importantly, the borrower, that the transaction occurred. Also, if you find yourself on the other end of the loan, when you pay someone back or bring back the lawn mower, get it in writing that the return was made. This prevents the other person from forgetting that you did, in fact, make the return.

Co-signors

If someone who is a friend or relative of the debtor co-signs an agreement, you can collect the debt from the co-signor when you find out the original debtor can't or won't pay. Having a co-signor also works as leverage against the original debtor, because most debtors would feel guilty if their friends or relatives end up on the hook for something they did.

Husband and Wife

Have them both sign, so both will be liable. Most states have laws that prevent creditors from taking assets owned jointly by a husband and wife, unless both have signed the agreement.

Don't Pay Cash

It's too easy to misplace the receipt and then not be able to prove that you bought the merchandise there, in the case of a purchase, or that you paid back the money you owed, in the case of a repair job or loan.

Warranties and Job Details

If these are in writing, then you can more easily enforce the original agreements in case of defective products or poor workmanship. Also, if you get it in writing, you will have a better idea from the beginning just what it is that you are getting. If you have questions about something, or the sales representative promises you something that isn't on paper, get it in writing then; don't wait until you get home and find out that what you paid for wasn't what you got.

Get Witnesses

Whether or not the agreement is in writing, if you have witnesses, especially friendly witnesses, you can verify what was agreed and what was said. This is true whether you are buying something or are in a car wreck. It's a good safeguard even when it's regarding an agreement as to when and how much payment will be received.

Know Your Debtor

Get the debtor's full name and address and phone and whatever other information you can. This is true for purchases, sales, car accidents, etc. Don't expect that someone will keep their word to you on something if you don't even know their name. The more you know about someone, the closer they might feel toward you and the more guilty they might also feel about cheating you. This is not true for everyone, but it can't hurt to try.

Evaluate his or her solvency. Does this person have a good job? Live in the neighborhood? Have other property and possessions that make him or her a good credit risk? For car accidents, make sure you get the name, telephone number, and as much other information as possible about the driver, witnesses, and insurance agent.

The more information you have about a person, a service, a happening, or a product, the better you can protect yourself from unforeseen problems.

Know Your "Big Brothers"

Often, government agencies or private consumer groups can come to your aid. For example, all new cars are covered by the Better Business Bureau's arbitration plan for just about any problem that could arise. Also, most states have extensive consumer services available through their offices of attorney general. These agencies are funded by your taxes, so you should avail yourself or their resources to help you solve a problem. They are especially helpful for consumer problems, including poor services, scam operations, housing, and the like.

In addition, the county attorney's offices can help prosecute some bad guys criminally. Although it's never legal to threaten someone with filing criminal charges if they don't pay a debt, it's always proper to report the deadbeat and let the law take over. Most states have bad check laws, although many do not strictly enforce them.

Deposits/Security

If you are a landlord or perform a service, such as painting, construction, or repair, you can always ask for money up front. If you loan someone some money or something else of value, you may use the same principle and ask the debtor to give you something of value as security or collateral.

If you are able to collect collateral against the debtor's loan, you have protected yourself the best way possible in case of a default. If the agreement is prepared properly, you should be able to keep the collateral, be it money or other property, because the debtor did not follow through with the agreement. These agreements can be forms, but check with your bank, credit union, or local attorney for the best form to use in your situation. Often, a dollar spent now will save you many dollars in the future.

If you have some type of security interest, often if the debtor files for bankruptcy, you will still be protected. You will not be paid by the debtor for the bill owed, but you will be able to cash in on the collateral or security interest attached to the bill.

Cash Only, No Checks

In God we trust, all others must pay cash. When paying for services, we advised you pay by check, but when you are collecting on a debt, demand cash payment. Too often, checks bounce better than basketballs. The laws relating to bad checks are sometimes so detailed that even if you know where the debtor lives, you won't be able to collect on a bad check. Also, usually the amount is so low it's not even worth your time, let alone an attorney's time, to go after a bad check. This rule is especially applicable when you don't know the person who is writing the check or if the check is drawn on an out-of-town bank.

Final Note

Stay organized, keep old receipts, bank checks, and all other records. The best offense in small claims court is to be prepared. Have all documents ready that relate to the specific claim. The judge is more inclined to believe written pieces of evidence than oral reiteration of facts.

Chapter 6

If Necessary, Choosing an Attorney

Choosing an attorney to take your case or to assist you may turn out to be the best strategy. The attorney you choose is also part of that strategy.

More and more, attorneys are becoming specialized in individual fields. A criminal attorney may not have the slightest idea how to handle a small claims case. In the larger metropolitan areas especially, debt collection has become a specialty. In most cases, because of the smaller dollar amount, these attorneys must do a large volume of cases to make this type of practice profitable. Because they are in court so often, on so many cases, they become experts at trial work and negotiation. But because most debts are so small, a lot of individual attention to your case is impossible.

Finding an Attorney

The methods of choosing an attorney include: the recommendation of business owners, bar association referrals, clubs, other attorneys, and referring to Martindale-Hubbell, *Law Directory*, a division of Reed Publishing (U.S.A.) Inc. (a multivolume set of listings for each state's attorneys).

The law is a learned profession. The more an attorney practices in an area, the better qualified he or she becomes. Typically, the more qualified the attorney, the more expensive the services. However, that attorney may be able to handle your case in half the time of the less experienced attorney. This is a judgment call where the recommendation of others comes in handy.

As a general rule, it is important to establish a rapport with a good general practice attorney. This attorney may be able to take your case or would surely give you a recommendation as to whom you should turn. Once you have established that you pay your bills, you may be able to avoid the retainer fee.

Methods of Payment

Collection cases are taken by attorneys under three forms of payment. The first method is the hourly rate. Often the attorney will request a retainer fee. This is a fee that is forwarded to the attorney before he or she begins work on the case. The hours spent on the case will typically be applied to the retainer. Be sure to get an estimate of the amount of money that will be necessary to complete the case.

The second method is payment contingient on the money being collected. Under this method, the attorney will not request any fee up front, other than incidental expenses, like filing and service fees. Upon successful completion of the case and collection of the money owed, the attorney will often take anywhere from 25-50 percent of the money. Whether you choose this method is a judgment call on your part. Talk to the attorney. Determine how much time this case is expected to take. Estimate the money expected to be collected and make your decision. If it is questionable whether you can get the judgment or whether you can collect the money once the judgment is received, it may be wise to hire the attorney on a percentage or contingency fee basis. If the case seems to be an easy win and it seems likely that the defendant will pay upon completion of the case, it may be wise to hire an attorney by the hour. Typical fees run from $75 to $100 per hour. Do not hesitate to ask about fees.

The third method is a flat fee arrangement. Under this method, the client is assured of the exact cost of the representation. Many attorneys are hesitant to use this method because of the variance of each case. Each case takes a different amount of research, negotiation, trial preparation, meetings with the client, and actual trial time. Each client demands different amounts of time. If you are hiring the attorney on an hourly basis, each time you make a call to the attorney to ask a question, you will probably be billed. It is a good idea to list all the questions needing answers and ask them at one time. This will keep your legal fees down.

The attorney, when sending a bill, will often send along a description of the charges. If you have a question concerning the billing, it is perfectly acceptable to ask what certain terms or work means.

You, as a client, have an obligation to your attorney. You have a duty to be candid about your case. Be outright and honest. Be complete in your story of the facts. Be prompt for appointments. Bring papers that are important to the case. Be organized. You have a duty to pay your attorney promptly. A client who pays his attorney on time is more apt to get prompt service in return.

Conclusion

No system is perfect. Expect justice, but don't expect it without exception, without doing your part, without some compromise, and without cost.

Knowledge and preparation are the keys to succeeding. If you have a valid claim, you are likely to prevail in this most civilized method of settling differences. The court is neutral by law and is charged with weighing the rights of the parties. The system is designed to be fair, inexpensive, and efficient.

Play by the rules of the court system. Remember, it is possible to lose a good case if you get careless. Take advantage of the strategies you have gained from this book. With a little bit of knowledge about the system, you are one step ahead of the game.

Chapter 7

State Court
Small Claims
Information

Overview

The information in this chapter is organized state-by-state. It includes details on monetary limitations, statutes of limitation, rules on who can act as a private process server, legal hotlines or information lines, the recourse a state allows when a defendant does not voluntarily pay a judgment, laws concerning garnishment of wages, property liens, and much more. Some of the information presented is so detailed that it could not be completely outlined here. Your clerk's office can give you complete and current information regarding your claim.

NOTE: BECAUSE OF EVER-CHANGING LAWS, PLEASE DOUBLE-CHECK ALL INFORMATION WITH YOUR LOCAL CLERK'S OFFICE

THIS INFORMATION IS FOR GENERAL REFERENCE ONLY AND IS *NOT* TO BE RELIED ON AS FINAL AUTHORITY.

Alabama

Name of Court: District Court

Dollar Limitation: $1,500 (exclusive of interest and costs)

Attorneys Allowed: Yes

Interest on Judgment: 12% or amount specified in contract

Statutory Filing Fee: $25 (Note: This fee may not include all costs involved in the individual county's filing fee. Additional fees for court automation, library, security, etc., are allowed.)

Statute of Limitation:

Most Contract Actions: 6 Years
Contract for Sale of Goods: 4 Years
Most Tort Actions: 20 Years
Judgments: 20 Years

Methods of Service of Process:

Individual

1. Sheriff or other officer in courts where debtor resides

2. Process server, at least 18 years old, appointed by the court

3. Certified mail

Corporation

Must serve registered agent

To obtain corporation information:

Secretary of State
Corporation Division
524 State Office Building
Montgomery, AL 36130
(205) 242-5324

Wage Garnishment Exemptions: 75% of wages exempt, employee can't waive exemption. Must file affidavit with clerk stating amount owing and that garnishment is necessary.

Homestead Exemption: $15,000 worth of equity—160 acres.

Personal Property Exemptions:

1. $3,000 worth of goods to be selected by debtor

2. Burial place

3. Church pew

4. Wearing apparel

5. Family pictures and books

Note: Debtor may waive exemption rights.

Judgment Lien on Real Estate: A judgment is not an automatic lien on the debtor's real estate. A certified copy of the judgment must be filed with the county clerk in each county where the debtor owns property to have a properly filed lien in that county.

Alaska

Name of Court: Small Claims Court

Dollar Limitation: $5,000 (exclusive of interest and costs)

Interest on Judgment: 10.5% or amount specified in contract

Statutory Filing Fee: $15 (Note: This fee may not include all costs involved in the individual county's filing fee. Additional fees for court automation, library, security, etc., are allowed.)

Statute of Limitation:

Most Contract Actions: 4 Years
Most Tort Actions: 2 Years
Judgments: 10 Years. However, if 5 years lapse without an execution being issued on the judgment, you must get court approval to obtain a writ of execution.

Methods of Service of Process:

Individual

1. Peace officer

2. Process server appointed by Commissioner of Public Safety

3. Where rule so provides, by registered or certified mail. Mailed by the clerk.

Corporation

Must serve registered agent

To obtain corporation information:

Department of Commerce and Economic Development
Division of B.S.C.
Attention: Corporation Section
P.O. Box D
Juneau, AK 99811

Wage Garnishment Rules: Garnishment is continuous until judgment is satisfied.

Wage Garnishment Exemptions: 25% of disposable wage or amount by which income exceeds $175/week or $700/month, whichever is less.

Homestead Exemption: $27,000 equity in a residence

Personal Property Exemptions:

1. Tools of trade, up to $1,400 value

2. Household goods, wearing apparel, family pictures and heirlooms, musical instruments, up to $1,500 value

3. Watches, jewelry, up to $500 value

4. Pets, up to $500 value

5. Automobile, up to $1,500 value

6. Burial plot

7. Necessary health aids

8. Certain liquor licenses

Judgment Lien on Real Estate: A judgment is not an automatic lien on debtor's real estate. A certified copy of the judgment must be filed with the recorder in each recording district where the debtor owns property to have a properly filed lien in that district.

Note: Mediation, conciliation, and arbitration services are available as alternatives to litigation.

Arizona

Name of Court: Small Claims Division of Justice of the Peace Court

Dollar Limitation: $1,000 (exclusive of interest and costs)

Subject Matter Limitation: The following cases are not allowed in this court:

1. Libel or slander claims

2. Forcible entry, forcible detainer, unlawful detainer actions

3. Specific performance actions

4. Class actions

5. Prejudgment remedies

6. Injunctive relief actions

7. Traffic violations

8. Criminal matters

9. Body attachment actions

Attorneys Allowed: Hearing is in front of hearing officer without attorneys present. If parties would like to use attorneys, the case can be transferred to the Justice Court.

Statutory Filing Fee: $3 (Note: This fee may not include all costs involved in the individual county's filing fee. Additional fees for court automation, library, security, etc., are allowed.)

Interest on Judgment: 10% or amount specified in contract

Statute of Limitation:

Most Contract Actions: 6 Years
Contract for Sale of Goods: 4 Years
Most Tort Actions: 1-2 Years
Real Estate Lien Judgment: 5 Years
Judgment Lien Filed with City Clerk: 5 Years from date of judgment
Renewable: Yes, by filing affidavit within 90 days of 5 year period

Methods of Service of Process:

Individual

1. Sheriff or deputy

2. Process server who is at least 21 years old and is registered with the clerk as a private process server (not the attorney or party to the case)

3. First class, registered or certified mail (Fee: $3)

Corporation

Must serve registered agent

To obtain corporation information:

Secretary of State
(602) 542-3026

Time for Defendant to Answer Complaint: 20 days (Fee: $2)

Time for Setting First Hearing: 30 days from time of filing defendant's answer. The clerk shall notify the parties of the hearing date and time.

Wage Garnishment Exemptions: Lesser of 25% of disposable earnings for each week, or amount by which disposable weekly earnings exceed 30 times federal minimum hourly wages.

Homestead Exemption: $100,000 equity in a residence

Personal Property Exemptions:

1. Tools of trade, not in excess of $2,500

2. Most personal items

3. Household furnishings, up to $4,000

    a. If married, each spouse is allowed the statutory exemptions: wearing apparel, food and fuel for 6 months, tools of trade up to $2,500

    b. Debtor can't waive exemptions

    c. The court may schedule hearings for evenings and Saturdays.

Judgment Lien on Real Estate: A judgment is not an automatic lien on debtor's real estate. A certified copy of the judgment must be filed with the county clerk in each county where the debtor owns property to have a properly filed lien in that county.

Helpful Numbers: Tell-LAW (602) 254-4099 (code #110 for small claims information) Lawyer Referal Service: (602) 257-4434

Note: Helpful brochures are available from many of the clerks' offices.

Arkansas

Name of Court: Small Claims Division of Municipal Court

Dollar Limitation: $3,000 (exclusive of interest and costs)

Interest Rate on Judgments: 10% or amount specified in contract

Attorneys Allowed: No, if a party wants legal counsel, case must be transferred to the regular municipal court docket.

Statutory Filing Fee: $5 (Note: This fee may not include all costs involved in the individual county's filing fee. Additional fees for court automation, library, security, etc., are allowed.)

Statute of Limitation:

Most Contract Actions: 5 Years for written and 3 Years for oral
Most Tort Actions: 3 Years for personal injury, 2 Years for medical malpractice
Judgments: 10 Years
Judgment Lien on Realty: 10 Years
Renewable: Yes

Methods of Service of Process:

Individual

1. Sheriff

2. Process server appointed by court

3. By mail as allowed by rules

Corporation

Must serve registered agent

To obtain corporation information:

Secretary of State
Corporation Division
State Capital
Little Rock, AR 72201
(501) 682-3441
(501) 682-5151

Wage Garnishment Rules: Can continue for 3 month periods.

Wage Garnishment Exemptions: First $25 of weekly net wages absolutely exempt.

Homestead Exemption: 1 acre in town or city or 160 acres in country in area.

Personal Property Exemptions:

1. $500 selected by debtor who is married and head of family

2. $200 for unmarried debtor

3. Wearing apparel

4. Insurance proceeds, up to $500

Note: Exemptions may not be waived in advance.

Judgment Lien on Real Estate: A judgment is an automatic lien on debtor's real estate in the county where the judgment was received.

California

Name of Court: Small Claims Court

Dollar Limitation: $5,000 (exclusive of interest and costs)

Interest Rate on Judgments: 10%

Attorneys Allowed: No, but legal advisors are available to parties at no charge, if requested. The extent of this service will vary from county to county, depending on local needs and conditions. These advisors may include volunteer attorneys, paralegals, and law students.

Statutory Filing Fee: $8 (Note: This fee may not include all costs involved in the individual county's filing fee. Additional fees for court automation, library, security, etc., are allowed.)

Statute of Limitation:

Most Contract Actions: 4 Years for written contracts, 2 Years for oral contracts
Most Tort Actions: 2-3 Years
Judgments: 10 Years
Renewable: Yes, by making an application for renewal with the court

Method of Service of Process:

Individual

1. Any person 18 years old who is not a party to the action

2. Certified or registered mail

Corporation

Must serve registered agent

To obtain corporation information:

Secretary of State
(916) 445-2900

Hearing Date: Set between 10 and 40 days from the date of judge's order for in-county defendant. Set between 30 and 70 days from the date of judge's order for out-of-county defendant.

Wage Garnishment Exemptions: 75% of wages is exempt

Homestead Exemption: $75,000 equity in a residence if debtor is 65 years old, disabled, or 55 years old with income less than $15,000/year; or, $45,000 equity in a residence if family member; or, $30,000 equity in a residence for all others.

Personal Property Exemptions:

1. Vehicle, up to $1,200

2. Household furnishings

3. Jewelry, art, up to $2,500

4. Tools of trade, up to $2,500

5. Deposit accounts, from $500 to $750

6. Retirement benefits

7. Unemployment benefits

8. Disability benefits

9. Financial aid

10. Cemetery plot

Notes:

a. Defendant can't waive exemptions.

b. No attachment allowed through small claims court unless specifically stated in judgment order.

c. The court can order installment payments be made by the defendant.

d. Once a judgment is entered, the clerk shall mail a notice of judgment to both parties. Attached is an information sheet the defendant is required to answer if he does not pay the judgment off in 35 days. If defendant fails to return the sheet, plaintiff may ask the court to impose penalties.

Judgment Lien on Real Estate: A judgment is not an automatic lien on debtor's real estate. A certified copy of the judgment, called an Abstract of Judgment, must be filed with the county clerk in each county where the debtor owns property to have a properly filed lien in that county.

Colorado

Name of Court: County Court—Small Claims Division

Dollar Limitation: $3,500 (exclusive of interest and costs)

Limitation on Amount of Claims Filed: A plaintiff may only file two claims per month or eighteen claims per year in small claims court.

Interest Rate on Judgments: 8% or amount specified in contract

Attorneys Allowed: No, if parties want attorney, must switch case to county court and there will be an additional docket fee.

Statutory Filing Fee: $17 (Note: This fee may not include all costs involved in the individual county's filing fee. Additional fees for court automation, library, security, etc., are allowed.)

Statute of Limitation:

Most Contract Actions: 3 Years for written, oral, and Uniform Commercial Code (UCC) Contracts
Most Tort Actions: 2 Years
Judgments: 6 Years
Judgment Lien on Realty: 6 Years
Renewable: Yes

Methods of Service of Process:

Individual

1. Sheriff or his deputy

2. Anyone over age 18, not a party to the action

3. Certified or registered mail

Corporation

Must serve registered agent

To obtain corporation information:

Secretary of State
(303) 894-2251

Wage Garnishment Rules: Continuous garnishment for up to 90 days; 2 copies of the writ must be served on garnishee, one copy sent to judgment debtor. Only one writ of continuing garnishment on wages may be placed in force at one time. The first writ served is the first writ to be satisfied.

Wage Garnishment Exemptions: Lesser of 25% of disposable earnings, or amount disposable earnings exceeds 30 times federal minimum hourly wage.

Homestead Exemption: $20,000 equity in a residence

Personal Property Exemptions:

1. Wearing apparel, up to $750 in value

2. Watches, Jewelry, etc., up to $500 in value

3. Family pictures and books, up to $750 in value

4. Burial site, one site for debtor and each dependent

5. Household furnishings, up to $1,500 in value

6. Tools of trade, up to $1,500 in value

7. Vehicle used for business or medical purposes, up to $3,000 in value

8. Certain pensions

9. Life insurance proceeds, up to $5,000 in value

10. Certain personal injury claims

Judgment Lien on Real Estate: A judgment is not an automatic lien on debtor's real estate. A certified copy of the judgment must be filed with the county recorder in each county where the debtor owns property to have a properly filed lien in that county.

Note: The clerk's office is required to publish a small claims court handbook, explaining the purpose of small claims court, the hours and procedures involved. Contact your local small claims clerk for information as to receiving a copy.

Connecticut

Name of Court: Small Claims Court

Dollar Limitation: $2,000 (exclusive of interest and costs)

Interest Rate on Judgments: 8% or amount specified in contract

Attorneys Allowed: Yes

Statutory Filing Fee: $20 for housing matters; $25 for all other matters (Note: This fee may not include all costs involved in the individual county's filing fee. Additional fees for court automation, library, security, etc., are allowed.)

Statute of Limitation:

Most Contract Actions: 6 Years for written, 3 Years for oral
Most Tort Actions: 3 Years for some, but mostly 2 Years, including medical malpractice, injuries resulting in death
Judgments: 15 Years
Renewable: Yes

Methods of Service of Process:

Individual

1. Regular mail (mailed by clerk)

2. If defendant does not answer the complaint within the time required, you will then have to hire a sheriff deputy or constable to deliver the complaint to the defendant.

Corporation

Must serve registered agent

To obtain corporation information:

Secretary of State
(203) 566-8570

Wage Garnishment Rules: Wage garnishment are allowed. Typical garnishments are set at $15.00 per week.

Homestead Exemption: No homestead laws in Connecticut

Personal Property Exemptions:

1. Necessities

2. Tools of trade

3. Burial plot

4. Public assistance payments

5. Health insurance payments

6. Disability payments

7. Certain benefits

8. Payments for child support

9. Motor vehicle, up to $1,500

10. Wedding and engagement rings

11. Certain pension plans

12. Alimony and support

Judgment Lien on Real Estate: A judgment is not an automatic lien on debtor's real estate. A certified copy of the judgment must be filed with the county clerk in each county where the debtor owns property to have a properly filed lien in that county.

Attorney Referral Service: (203) 525-6052

Note: A pamphlet entitled "A Guide to the Use of Connecticut Small Claims Courts," published by the Connecticut Bar Association, is available from your local clerk's office.

Delaware

Name of Court: Justice of the Peace Courts

Dollar Limitation: $5,000 (exclusive of interest and costs)

Interest Rate on Judgments: 5% over Federal Reserve discount

Attorneys Allowed: Yes

Statutory Filing Fee: $16 (Note: This fee may not include all costs involved in the individual county's filing fee. Additional fees for court automation, library, security, etc., are allowed.)

Statute of Limitation:

> Most Contract Actions: 4 Years for sale of goods, 3 Years for written and oral contracts
> Most Tort Actions: 2 Years
> Judgments: 10 Years (on land)
> Renewable: Yes

Methods of Service of Process:

Individual

1. Sheriff, coroner, constable, deputy sheriff

Note: A copy of a praecipe shall accompany each summons.

Corporation

Must serve registered agent

To obtain corporation information:

> Secretary of State
> (302) 739-3073

Wage Garnishment Rules: Exemption can't be waived

Wage Garnishment Exemptions: 85% of wages are exempt, attaches to wages until entire claim is paid

Homestead Exemption: No homestead laws in Delaware

Personal Property Exemptions:

1. Family books and pictures

2. Church pews

3. Burial plot

4. Wearing apparel

5. Tools of trade (only exempt to $75 in New Castle and Sussex Counties, and $50 in Kent County)

6. Sewing machine

7. Piano

8. Most benefits

Judgment Lien on Real Estate: A judgment is not an automatic lien on debtor's real estate. A certified copy of the judgment must be filed with the county clerk in each county where the debtor owns property to have a properly filed lien in that county.

District of Columbia

Name of Court: Superior Court Small Claims Court

Address: 500 Indiana Avenue, N.W.
John Marshall Level, Room JM-260
Washington, D.C. 20001
(202) 879-1120

Dollar Limitation: $2,000 (exclusive of interest and costs)

Interest Rate on Judgments: Contractual rate or amount specified by Secretary of Treasury

Attorneys Allowed: Yes. Corporations must be represented by an attorney.

Statutory Filing Fee: $1 (Note: This fee may not include all costs involved in the individual county's filing fee. Additional fees for court automation, library, security, etc., are allowed.)

Statute of Limitation:

Most Contract Actions: 4 Years for sale of goods, 3 Years for express or implied simple contracts
Most Tort Actions: 1 Year
Lien on Real Estate Judgments: 12 Years
Renewable: Yes

Methods of Service of Process:

Individual

1. U.S. Marshal

2. Any person 18 years old who is not a party to the action

3. Certified or registered mail

4. 1st class mail, with 2 copies of Form 1-A, notice and acknowledgement for service by mail, including SASE

Corporation

Must serve registered agent

To obtain corporation information:

> Secretary of State
> (202) 727-7283

Wage Garnishment Rules: Continuing writ for either

Wage Garnishment Exemptions: 25% of disposable earnings amount by which disposable wages exceed 30 times federal minimum wage, whichever is less.

Homestead Exemption: No homestead laws in D.C.

Personal Property Exemptions:

1. Wearing apparel, up to $300

2. Household furnishings

3. Mechanics tools, up to $200

4. Disability and life insurance benefits

5. Public assistance and unemployment compensation

Note: Debtor can't waive exemptions

Note: Mediation is available.

Multi-Door Dispute Resolution Program
Room C-500
D.C. Courthouse
500 Indiana Avenue, N.W.
Washington, D.C. 20001
(202) 879-1549
Hours: 9:00 a.m. - 4:00 p.m.

If you need help with your case:

Columbus Community Legal Services
1713 North Capitol Street, N.E.
Washington, D.C. 20002
(202) 526-5800

D.C. Law Students In Court Program
419 Seventh Street, N.W., Suite 202
Washington, D.C. 20004
(202) 638-4798

Legal Aid Society
666 Eleventh Street, N.W., Suite 300
Washington, D.C. 20001
(202) 727-1785

Neighborhood Legal Services
310 Sixth Street, N.W.
Washington, D.C. 20001
(202) 628-9161

Lawyer Referral: (202) 331-4365

Florida

Name of Court: County Court, Summary Procedure Division

Dollar Limitation: $2,500 (exclusive of interest, costs and attorney's fees)

Interest Rate on Judgments: 12%

Attorneys Allowed: Yes

Statutory Filing Fee: $10.00 on claims below $100.00, $25.00 on claims above $100.00. (Note: This fee may not include all costs involved in the individual county's filing fee. Additional fees for court automation, library, security, etc., are allowed.)

Statute of Limitation:

Most Contract Actions: 5 Years
Most Tort Actions: 4 Years
Judgments: 7 Years
Renewable: Yes
Judgment Lien on Real Estate: 7 Years

Methods of Service of Process:

Individual

1. Sheriff

2. Special process server

3. Certified mail

Corporation

Must serve registered agent or highest ranking officer of corporation available.

To obtain corporation information:

Secretary of State
(904) 488-9000

Garnishment Rules: Bank accounts cannot be garnished if amount can be traced back to head of household's earnings.

Wage Garnishment Exemptions: Head of household and government employees are exempt from wage garnishments.

Homestead Exemption: 1/2 acre in a municipality or 160 contiguous acres outside a municipality.

Personal Property Exemptions:

1. $1,000 of personal property

2. Disability income benefits

3. Cash surrender value of life insurance policies

4. Life insurance proceeds

Judgment Lien on Real Estate: A judgment is not an automatic lien on debtor's real estate. A certified copy of the judgment must be filed with the county clerk in each county where the debtor owns property to have a properly filed lien in that county.

Note: Information on Florida law and procedure is available through a program sponsored by the Florida Bar: Florida Call-A-Law (904) 561-1200.

Florida Attorney Referral Service: (800) 342-8011

Georgia

Name of Court: Magistrate Courts

Dollar Limitation: $5,000 (exclusive of interest and costs)

Interest Rate on Judgments: 12% or amount specified in contract

Attorneys Allowed: Yes

Statutory Filing Fee: $40 (includes Marshall's service)

Statute of Limitation:

Most Contract Actions: For written, 5 Years, for oral, 4 Years
Most Tort Actions: 2-5 Years, depending on action
Judgments: 7 Years
Renewable: Yes

Methods of Service of Process:

Individual

1. Sheriff

2. Marshall of court

3. Deputy

4. Any other U.S. citizen appointed by court

Corporation

Must serve registered agent

To obtain corporation information:

Secretary of State
(404) 656-2817

Note: Defendant has 45 days to answer the complaint or the court will issue a default in Plaintiff's favor.

Wage Garnishment Rules: Continuing until paid in full.

Wage Garnishment Exemptions: Lesser of 25% of disposable earnings, or amount disposable earnings exceeds 30 times federal minimum hourly wage.

Homestead Exemption: $5,000 equity in a residence

Personal Property Exemptions: Waiver of exemptions allowed, except for wearing apparel and $300 of household furnishings, to be chosen by defendant.

Judgment Lien on Real Estate: A judgment is not an automatic lien on debtor's real estate. A certified copy of the judgment must be filed with the county clerk in each county where the debtor owns property, and must be recorded on general execution docket.

Note: Once judgment is received, the judge can order the defendant to make payments and order that no post-garnishment proceedings, such as wage garnishments, be done if the payments are made in a timely manner.

Small Claims Information (Fulton County): (404) 730-5000

Hawaii

Name of Court: Small Claims Division of District Court

Dollar Limitation: $2,500 (exclusive of interest and costs)

Interest Rate on Judgments: 10%

Attorneys Allowed: Yes, except in landlord-tenant cases.

Statutory Filing Fee: $5 (Note: This fee may not include all costs involved in the individual county's filing fee. Additional fees for court automation, library, security, etc. are allowed.)

Statute of Limitation:

Most Contract Actions: 4 Years
Most Tort Actions: 2 Years
Judgments: 10 Years
Lien on Real Estate: 10 Years

Methods of Service of Process:

Individual

1. Registered mail, certified mail with return receipt

2. Sheriff, deputy, chief of police

3. Person appointed by court

4. Licensed process server

Corporation

Must serve corporate officer or registered agent

To obtain corporation information:

Secretary of State
(808) 586-2727

Wage Garnishment Rules: Continuing writ

Wage Garnishment Property Which May Be Reached: 5% of first $100/month, 10% of next $100, 20% of excess.

Homestead Exemption: $20,000/$30,000 equity in a residence for head of household or person 65 or older.

Personal Property Exemptions:

1. Life insurance

2. State pensions

3. Some benefits

Judgment Lien on Real Estate: A judgment is not an automatic lien on debtor's real estate. A certified copy of the judgment must be filed with the clerk of the court where entered and recorded in the bureau of conveyances to be a properly filed lien.

Note: The clerk, at the plaintiff's request will prepare the papers necessary to be filed in the action. This service is not available to a sole proprietorship, partnership, or corporation.

Idaho

Name of Court: Small Claims Department of the Magistrate's Division

Dollar Limitation: $2,000 (exclusive of interest and costs)

Interest Rate on Judgments: 5% above annual yield on U.S. Treasury Securities

Attorneys Allowed: No

Statutory Filing Fee: $18 (Note: This fee may not include all costs involved in the individual county's filing fee. Additional fees for court automation, library, security, etc. are allowed.)

Statute of Limitation:

Most Contract Actions: 5 Years for written, 4 Years for oral
Most Tort Actions: 2 Years
Judgments: 6 Years
Lien on Property: 2 Years
Renewable: Yes, upon petition and order from judge, for 2 Years

Methods of Service of Process:

Individual

1. Sheriff, deputy, or constable

2. Any person over 18 years old, not a party to action

Corporation

Must serve registered agent or director

To obtain corporation information:

Secretary of State
(208) 334-2300

Wage Garnishment Rules: No attachment or garnishment may issue until judgment is recorded.

Wage Garnishment Exemptions: Lesser of 25% of disposable earnings, or amount of disposable earnings exceeding 40 times federal minimum hourly wage.

Homestead Exemption: $25,000 equity in a residence

Personal Property Exemptions:

1. Burial plot

2. Necessary health aids

3. Social Security and Veteran's benefits

4. Unemployment compensation

5. Alimony, Maintenance

6. Public assistance

7. Proceeds for some insurance and judgment settlements for bodily injury

8. Property to the extent reasonably necessary for the support of the debtor and his dependents

9. Of the following, up to $500 value in any one item, not exceeding $4,000 total exemption:

   a. household furnishings, including one firearm

   b. wearing apparel, books, pets, musical instruments

   c. jewelry, $250 value

   d. tools of trade, $1,000 value

   e. vehicle, $1,500 value

Judgment Lien on Real Estate: A judgment is not an automatic lien on debtor's real estate. A certified copy of the judgment must be filed with the county clerk in each county where the debtor owns property to have a properly filed lien in that county.

Illinois

Name of Court: Small Claims Court

Dollar Limitation: $2,500 (exclusive of interest and costs)

Interest Rate on Judgments: 9% or amount specified in contract

Attorneys Allowed: Yes

Statutory Filing Fee: $10 for claims up to $500, $25 for claims up to $2,500 (Note: This fee may not include all costs involved in the individual county's filing fee. Additional fees for court automation, library, security, etc. are allowed.)

Statute of Limitation:

Most Contract Actions: 10 Years for written, 5 Years for oral, 4 Years for UCC, 5 Years for property damage.
Most Tort Actions: 2 Years
Judgments: 7 Years
Renewable: In some cases, yes, up to 20 Years

Methods of Service of Process:

Individual

1. Sheriff or deputy

2. Process server over age 18 upon motion and order of court

3. Licensed private investigator.

4. Certified mail if debtor resides within county where suit is filed

Corporation

Must serve registered agent or any officer or agent found within the state

To obtain corporation information:

> Secretary of State
> Office of Corporations Department
> 3rd Floor
> Centennial Building
> Springfield, IL 62756
> (217) 782-6875
> (217) 782-7880

They will answer questions over the phone. To receive written listing of a corporation's information, send $15 with request.

Wage Garnishment Rules: Liberally allowed. Each writ of garnishment continues for eight week period. Another writ must be issued if a balance on the judgment remains.

Wage Garnishment Exemptions: Lesser of 15% of gross earnings, or amount of disposable earnings exceeding 40 times federal minimum hourly wage.

Homestead Exemption: $7,500 worth of equity in a home which the debtor is occupying.

Personal Property Exemptions:

1. Wearing apparel

2. Family books

3. Equity interest not exceeding $2,000

4. One Vehicle, up to $1,200 value

5. Tools of trade, up to $750 equity value

6. Life insurance benefits

7. Other benefits, e.g., wrongful death, welfare, social security, unemployment

8. Alimony

Judgment Lien on Real Estate: A judgment is not an automatic lien on debtor's real estate. A certified copy of the judgment must be filed with the county clerk in each county where the debtor owns property to have a properly filed lien in that county.

Indiana

Name of Court: Small Claims Court

Dollar Limitation: $3,000 (exclusive of interest and costs)

Interest Rate on Judgments: 10% or amount specified in contract if contract states lower percentage

Attorneys Allowed: Yes

Statutory Filing Fee: $22 (Note: This fee includes payment for service of process by registered or certified mail, but may not include all costs involved in the individual county's filing fee. Additional fees for court automation, library, security, etc., are allowed.)

Statute of Limitation:

Most Contract Actions: For written, 20 Years if entered into before 9/1/82, or 10 Years if entered into after 8/31/82, for oral, 6 Years
Contract for Sale of Goods: 4 Years
Most Tort Actions: 2 Years
Judgment Lien on Real Estate: 10 Years

Methods of Service of Process:

Individual

1. Sheriff or deputy

2. Person appointed by court

3. Mail (return receipt requested and returned showing receipt)

Corporation

Must serve registered agent

To obtain corporation information:

Secretary of State
(317) 232-6531

Wage Garnishment Rules: Plaintiff files an affidavit and bond, clerk issues summons.

Wage Garnishment Exemptions: Lesser of 25% of disposable earnings, or amount disposable earnings exceed 30 times federal minimum hourly wage.

Homestead Exemption: $7,500 equity in a residence

Personal Property Exemptions:

1. Personal property, up to $4,000

2. Intangible personal property, up to $100

3. Health aids

4. Real estate held as tenants by entirety

5. Pension and retirement funds and accounts

Judgment Lien on Real Estate: A judgment is not an automatic lien on debtor's real estate. A certified copy of the judgment must be filed with the county clerk in docket books in each county where the debtor owns property to have a properly filed lien in that county.

Iowa

Name of Court: Small Claims Court

Dollar Limitation: $2,000 (exclusive of interest and costs)

Interest Rate on Judgments: 10% or amount specified in contract

Attorneys Allowed: Yes

Statutory Filing Fee: $15 (Note: This fee may not include all costs involved in the individual county's filing fee. Additional fees for court automation, library, security, etc., are allowed.)

Statute of Limitation:

Most Contract Actions: 10 Years for written, 5 Years for oral
Most Tort Actions: 2 Years
Judgments: 20 Years
Lien on Real Estate: 10 Years

Note: Any action on judgement can't be brought after 20 years

Methods of Service of Process:

Individual

1. Certified mail

2. Restricted delivery

3. Peace Officer

4. Any person approved by the court

Corporation

Must serve registered agent

To obtain corporation information:

Secretary of State
(515) 281-5864

Wage Garnishment Rules: Court may provide for installment payments to avoid garnishment

Wage Garnishment Exemptions: If debtor only has $12,000 or less earnings per year, no more than $250 can be garnished.

Homestead Exemption: 1/2 acre in city, or 40 acres outside, or $500 value, whichever is greater.

Personal Property Exemptions:

1. Wearing apparel, up to $1,000

2. 1 shotgun and 1 rifle or musket

3. Family books and pictures, up to $1,000

4. Burial plot

5. Household furnishings, up to $2,000

6. Certain insurance policies and benefit plans

7. Alimony and support

8. Tools of trade, up to $10,000

9. Up to $5,000 of: vehicles, musical instruments, certain tax refunds

Judgment Lien on Real Estate: Judgment is a lien on any real property of the debtor within the county. Must specially file copy of judgment in any other county court in Iowa. Judgment is lien on real estate once entered in lien index of clerk of court.

Kansas

Name of Court: Kansas Small Claims Court

Dollar Limitation: $500 (exclusive of interest and costs)

Filing Limitation: Plaintiff may only file 5 claims per year in small claims court

Interest Rate on Judgments: 4% above the discount rate. Changes yearly.

Attorneys Allowed: Only for post-judgment actions

Statutory Filing Fee: $10 (Note: This fee may not include all costs involved in the individual county's filing fee. Additional fees for court automation, library, security, etc., are allowed.)

Statute of Limitation:

Most Contract Actions: 5 Years for written, 3 Years for oral
Contract for Sale of Goods: 4 Years
Most Tort Actions: 2 Years
Judgments: 5 Years
Lien on Property: 5 Years
Renewable: Yes, if holder of lien within two years of the time the judgment becomes dormant files a motion for reviver and the motion is granted

Methods of Service of Process:

Individual

1. Sheriff

2. Certified mail

3. Private Process Server

Corporation

Must serve resident agent/ registered office

To obtain corporation information:

Secretary of State
Capital Building, 2nd Floor
Topeka, KS 66612-1594
(913) 296-2236

Wage Garnishment Rules: Garnishment continues until paid in full.

Wage Garnishment Exemptions: The employer is instructed to pay the employee the following, with the remainder being deducted to satisfy the judgment.

If wages are between (wkly):	Then pay the employee:
$1.00 and $79.49	the full amount
$79.50 and $106.00	$79.50
More than $106.00	75% of disposable earnings

Homestead Exemption: 1 acre in city, 160 acres outside incorporated area.

Personal Property Exemptions:

1. Household furnishings

2. Jewelry, up to $500

3. 1 vehicle

4. Cemetery plot

5. Family books, furniture, tools of trade, up to $5,000

Note: Once judgment is received, clerk sends defendant a form that requests a list of all assets and place of employment. This must be completed and returned to court within 30 days.

Judgment Lien on Real Estate: A judgment is not an automatic lien on debtor's real estate. A certified copy of the judgment must be filed with the county clerk in each county where the debtor owns property to have a properly filed lien in that county.

Kentucky

Name of Court: Small Claims Court

Dollar Limitation: $1,000 (exclusive of interest and costs)

Filing Limitation: Plaintiff can only file 25 claims per year in small claims court.

Interest Rate on Judgments: 12%

Attorneys Allowed: Yes

Statutory Filing Fee: $15 for claims of $500 or less, $30 for claims of $500 or greater (Note: This fee may not include all costs involved in the individual county's filing fee. Additional fees for court automation, library, security, etc., are allowed.)

Statute of Limitation:

Most Contract Actions: 15 Years for written, 5 Years for oral
Most Tort Actions: Some 1, 2, 5, or 8 Years, depending on the action
Judgments: 15 Years

Methods of Service of Process:

Individual

1. Certified mail (return receipt requested)

2. County sheriff or any person appointed by sheriff

3. Specified bailiff appointed by court to serve process

Corporation

Must serve registered agent

To obtain corporation information:

Secretary of State
(502) 564-7330

Note: The hearing date is set 20-40 days after defendant is served.

Wage Garnishment Exemptions: Lesser of 25% of disposable earnings, or amount disposable earnings exceed 30 times federal minimum hourly wage.

Homestead Exemption: $5,000 equity in a residence

Personal Property Exemptions:

1. Household furnishings, jewelry, wearing apparel, up to $3,000 value

2. Tools of trade

3. Vehicle, up to $2,500 value

4. Health aids

5. Pensions, benefits

Judgment Lien on Real Estate: A judgment is not an automatic lien on debtor's real estate. A certified copy of the judgment must be filed with the county clerk in each county where the debtor owns property to have a properly filed lien in that county. The plaintiff must send notice of lien to defendant by 1st class mail.

Note: The attorney general is responsible for preparing and circulating a pamphlet to all circuit clerks concerning the rights and responsibilities of each party written in layman's language. The pamphlet details the steps required to follow through with the court process. Plaintiff can pick up a copy at the time he or she files the action. Defendant should receive a copy with the service.

Louisiana

Name of Court: Justice of Peace Court

Dollar Limitation: $2,000 (exclusive of interest and costs)

Interest Rate on Judgments: 12%

Attorneys Allowed: Yes

Statutory Filing Fee: $35 (Note: This fee may not include all costs involved in the individual county's filing fee. Additional fees for court automation, library, security, etc., are allowed.)

Statute of Limitation:

Most Contract Actions: 3 Years
Most Tort Actions: 1 Year
Judgments: 10 Years
Judgments on Real Estate Liens: 10 Years
Renewable: Yes

Methods of Service of Process:

Individual

Sheriff, or if sheriff can't or doesn't complete within 5 days, may use constable or party appointed by court

Corporation

Must serve registered agent

To obtain corporation information:

Secretary of State
(504) 925-4704

Wage Garnishment Rules: Requires a hearing to establish the exemption part of wages.

Wage Garnishment Exemptions: Lesser of 25% of disposable earnings, or amount disposable earnings exceed 30 times federal minimum hourly wage.

Homestead Exemption: 160 acres, which includes buildings and appurtenances, with $15,000 value.

Personal Property Exemptions:

1. Tools of trade

2. Wedding rings, up to $5,000

3. Household furnishings

4. Family portraits

5. Musical instruments

Judgment Lien on Real Estate: A judgment is not an automatic lien on debtor's real estate. A certified copy of the judgment must be filed with the county clerk in each county where the debtor owns property to have a properly filed lien in that county. A judgment isn't a lien on real estate in the county until it is recorded as a mortgage.

Maine

Name of Court: Small Claims Court

Dollar Limitation: $1,400 (exclusive of interest and costs)

Interest Rate on Judgments: 8%

Attorneys Allowed: Yes

Statutory Filing Fee: $5 (Note: This fee may not include all costs involved in the individual county's filing fee. Additional fees for court automation, library, security, etc., are allowed.)

Statute of Limitation:

Most Contract Actions: 6 Years
Most Tort Actions: 3 Years
Judgments: 20 Years

Methods of Service of Process:

Individual

1. Sheriff

2. Deputy Sheriff

3. Specially appointed process server

Corporation

Must serve registered agent

To obtain corporation information:

Secretary of State
(207) 289-3501

Wage Garnishment Exemptions: Wage garnishments are allowed, check with your local clerk for the exemptions.

Homestead Exemption: $7,500 or $60,000 equity in a residence if the debtor is over 60 years of age or physically or mentally handicapped and because of this disability, the debtor is unable to work.

Personal Property Exemption:

1. One vehicle, up to $1,200 value

2. Household furnishings, wearing apparel, books, animals, crops and musical instruments, up to $200 per item value

3. Jewelry, up to $500 value, and wedding and engagement ring

4. Tools of Trade, up to $1,000 value

5. Furnace, stove, and fuel

6. Food, produce, and animals

7. Farming equipment

8. Fishing boat, if used for commercial purposes

9. Unmatured life insurance policies

10. Life insurance dividends, interest, and loan value, up to $4,000 value

11. Health aids

12. Disability benefits and pensions

13. Some legal awards and life insurance benefits

14. Other property, $400 value

Judgment Lien on Real Estate: A judgment is not an automatic lien on debtor's real estate. A certified copy of the judgment must be filed in registry of deeds in each county where the debtor owns property to have a properly filed lien in that county. Must send notice by certified mail to debtor.

Maryland

Name of Court: District Court

Dollar Limitation: $10,000 (exclusive of interest and costs)

Interest Rate on Judgments: Legal rate or amount specified in contract

Attorneys Allowed: Yes

Statutory Filing Fee: $5 for claims $2,500 or less, $10 for claims $2,500 to $10,000

Statute of Limitation:

Most Contract Actions: 4 Years for sale of goods, 3 Years for governmental contracts
Most Tort Actions: 3 Years
Judgments: 12 Years

Methods of Service of Process:

Individual

1. Sheriff

2. Deputy sheriff

3. Competent person over 18 years old, not a party to action

4. Attorney of record

Note: Only sheriff or deputy sheriff can serve writs of execution, replevin, and attachment

Corporation

Must serve registered agent

To obtain corporation information:

Secretary of State
(301) 225-1330

Wage Garnishment Exemptions: The greater of $145/week or 75% of net wages. Caroline, Kent, Queen Annes, Worchester Counties: lesser of 25% of disposable earnings, or amount disposable earnings exceed 30 times federal minimum hourly wage.

Homestead Exemption: No homestead exemptions in Maryland

Personal Property Exemptions:

1. $3,000 cash or property selected by debtor

2. Wearing apparel

3. Books

4. Tools of trade, up to $2,500

5. Disability and other benefits

6. Certain retirement plans

7. Health aids, up to $500

Judgment Lien on Real Estate: A judgment is not an automatic lien on debtor's real estate. A certified copy of the judgment must be indexed and recorded in each county where the debtor owns property to have a properly filed lien in that county.

Legal Line: (800) 638-8862

Massachusetts

Name of Court: District Court

Dollar Limitation: $1,500 (exclusive of interest and costs)

Interest Rate on Judgments: Court will direct

Attorneys Allowed: Subject to judge's discretion as to extent

Statutory Filing Fee: $10 for claims $500 or less, $15 for claims $500 or greater (Note: This fee may not include all costs involved in the individual county's filing fee. Additional fees for court automation, library, security, etc., are allowed.)

Statute of Limitation:

Most Contract Actions: 6 Years
Most Tort Actions: Some 2 Years, some 3 Years

Methods of Service of Process:

Individual

1. Registered mail

2. Sheriff

3. Deputy sheriff

4. Any other person authorized by the court

Corporation

Must serve registered agent

To obtain corporation information:

Secretary of State
(617) 727-9640

Wage Garnishment Rules: Must notify debtor and court must give permission.

Wage Garnishment Exemptions: $125/week

Homestead Exemption: $100,000 value, or $200,000 for person 65 or older or disabled.

Personal Property Exemptions:

A certain value in the following:

1. Wearing apparel

2. Household goods

3. Livestock

4. Tools of trade

5. Motor vehicle

6. Savings deposit

7. Back wages for labor

Judgment Lien on Real Estate: A judgment is not an automatic lien on debtor's real estate. A certified copy of the judgment must be filed with the county clerk in each county where the debtor owns property to have a properly filed lien in that county.

Legal Advocacy: (617) 742-9179

Michigan

Name of Court: District Court

Dollar Limitation: $1,500 (exclusive of interest and costs)

Interest Rate on Judgements: 12%

Attorneys Allowed: No

Statutory Filing Fee: $12 (Note: This fee may not include all costs involved in the individual county's filing fee. Additional fees for court automation, library, security, etc., are allowed.)

Statute of Limitation:

Most Contract Actions: 6 Years
Action on Contract for Sale of Goods: 4 Years
Most Tort Actions: Usually 3 Years, some 2 Years

Methods of Service of Process:

Individual

1. Any person of age, not a party to the action

Corporation

Must serve registered agent

To obtain corporation information:

Michigan Department of Commerce
Corporation and Securities Bureau, Corporation Division
P.O. Box 30054
Lansing, MI 48909
(517) 334-6304

No charge for information given in writing or over the phone.

Wage Garnishment Exemptions: 25% of net pay is exempt; debtor must earn minimum $100/week before garnishment can be implemented.

Homestead Exemption: $3,500 in value and must be no greater than 1 lot (single parcel) in a city or 40 acres in unincorporated area.

Personal Property Exemptions:

1. Family pictures

2. Wearing Apparel

3. Household goods, up to $1,000

4. Church pew

5. Cemetery plot

6. Various farm animals

7. Tools of trade, up to $1,000

8. Certain disability benefits

9. IRA

Judgment Lien on Real Estate: A judgment is not an automatic lien on debtor's real estate. A certified copy of the judgment must be filed with the county clerk in each county where the debtor owns property to have a properly filed lien in that county.

Minnesota

Name of Court: Conciliation Court

Dollar Limitation: $4,000 or $2,000 when claim involves consumer credit transaction (exclusive of interest and costs)

Interest Rate on Judgments: Varies from year to year, generally somewhere between 6% and 11%.

Statutory Filing Fee: $5-15 (Note: This fee may not include all costs involved in the individual county's filing fee. Additional fees for court automation, library, security, etc., are allowed.)

Statute of Limitation:

> Most Contract Actions: 6 Years
> Most Tort Actions: 2 Years
> Judgments: 10 Years (Lien on property 10 years)
> Renewable: Yes, for another 10 Years

Methods of Service of Process:

Individual

1. Sheriff

2. Any person 18 or older not a party to the action

Corporation

Must serve corporation at address listed. Can serve registered agent, an officer or director.

To obtain corporation information:

> Secretary of State
> (612) 296-2803

Wage Garnishment Exemptions: Lesser of 25% of disposable earnings, or amount disposable earnings exceed 40 times federal minimum hourly wage.

Homestead Exemption: 1/2 acre within the city or 160 areas outside city.

Personal Property Exemptions:

1. Family books

2. Musical instruments

3. Pew in church burial plot

4. Wearing apparel

5. Household furnishings not exceeding $5,400 value

6. Motor vehicle ($2,000 value if farmer; $13,000 value in machines and implements

7. Tools of trade up to $5,000 value

Judgment Lien on Real Estate: A judgment is an automatic lien on all of defendant's real property within the county.

Mississippi

Name of Court: Justice Court

Dollar Limitation: $1,000 (exclusive of interest and costs)

Interest Rate on Judgments: Determined by judge at per annum rate or if there was an interest provision in the contract, then that applies.

Statutory Filing Fee: $34

Statute of Limitation:

>Most Contract Actions: 6 Years for contract for sale of goods, 3 Years for oral contract.
>Most Tort Actions: 1-2 Years
>Judgments: 7 Years

Methods of Service of Process:

Individual

1. Sheriff

2. Any person 18 years or older, not a party to the action

Corporation

Must serve registered agent

To obtain corporation information:

>Secretary of State
>(601) 359-1633

Wage Garnishment Exemptions: Lesser of 25% of disposable earnings, or amount by which disposable earnings exceed 30 times federal minimum hourly wage.

Homestead Exemption: $30,000 in value or 160 acres plus $250 worth of personal property.

Personal Property Exemptions:

1. $10,000 in tangible property to be selected by debtor

2. Insurance proceeds

3. Disability insurance

4. Alimony and child support

5. Proceeds from a judgment for injuries to debtor up to $10,000

Judgment Lien on Real Estate: A judgment is not an automatic lien on debtor's real estate. A certified copy of the judgment must be filed with the county clerk in each county where the debtor owns property.

Missouri

Name of Court: Small Claims Court

Dollar Limitation: $1,500 (exclusive of interest and costs)

Filing Limitation: Can only file six actions per year

Interest Rate on Judgments: 9% or amount agreed to in contract

Attorneys Allowed: Yes

Statutory Filing Fee: $10 for claims $100 to $1,500, $5 for claims up to $100 (Note: This fee may not include all costs involved in the individual county's filing fee. Additional fees for court automation, library, security, etc., are allowed.)

Statute of Limitation:

Most Contract Actions: 5 Years, 4 Years for contract for sale of goods
Most Tort Actions: 2 Years
Judgments: 10 Years

Methods of Service of Process:

Individual

1. Certified mail return receipt requested; if not successful, then,

2. Sheriff or his deputy

3. Coroner or specially appointed process server

Corporation

Must serve registered agent

To obtain corporation information:

Secretary of State, Corporation Division
P.O. Box 778
Jefferson City, MO 65102

To get a list of officers, request must be in writing, along with $5.

Wage Garnishment Exemptions: Lesser of 25% of disposable earnings, amount by which disposable earnings exceed 30 times federal minimum hourly wage, or 10% if employee is the head of household and state resident, whichever of the three is lesser.

Homestead Exemption: $8,000 equity in a residence

Personal Property Exemptions:

1. Household furnishings, up to $1,000 value

2. Jewelry, up to $500 value

3. Other property, up to $400 value

4. Tools of trade, up to $2,000 value

5. Motor vehicle, up to $500 value

6. Mobile home if that is the residence, up to $1,000 value

7. Life insurance and health aids

8. Some benefits and pension plans

9. Alimony, up to $500

Judgment Lien on Real Estate: A judgment obtained in a small claims court shall not be a lien on real estate.

Legal Assistance: (800) 392-8777 or (314) 635-4128

Notes: A self-explanatory pamplet on small claims court is available from the Missouri Bar by calling the numbers listed above.

Montana

Name of Court: Small Claims Court

Dollar Limitation: $2,500 (exclusive of interest and costs)

Filing Limitation: May file only 10 complaints per year

Interest Rate on Judgments: 10% or amount specified in contract

Attorneys Allowed: No, unless all parties are represented by attorneys

Statutory Filing Fee: $10

Statute of Limitation:

Most Contract Actions: 8 Years, 4 Years for contract for sale of goods
Most Tort Actions: 2-3 Years
Judgments: 10 Years
Judgment Lien on Real Estate: 6 Years

Methods of Service of Process:

Individual

1. Sheriff or Deputy

2. Constable or person over 18 not party to action (does not have to be specially appointed by a judge

Corporation

Must serve registered agent

To obtain corporation information:

Secretary of State
(406) 444-2034

Wage Garnishment Exemptions: Lesser of 25% of disposable earnings, or amount disposable earnings exceed 30 times federal minimum hourly wage.

Homestead Exemption: $40,000—limitation of value. 1/4 acre in town, 4 acres nonagricultural land not in town or 320 acres of agricultural land—limitation of area.

Personal Property Exemptions:

1. Professional prescribed health aids

2. Social security or public assistance benefits

3. Some veteran's benefits

4. Disability benefits

5. Maintenance and child support

6. Burial plots for family

7. Household furnishings, jewelry, wearing apparel, books, firearms, animals, feed, and musical instruments, each item not exceeding $600 value, with $4,500 aggregate value

8. One motor vehicle, $1,200 value

9. Tools of the trade, $3,000 value

10. Interest in unmatured life insurance contracts, $4,000 value

Judgment Lien on Real Estate: A judgment is a lien on real estate within the county. Must certify a copy of judgment with other counties' clerks to get a lien then.

Note: Court has a pamphlet explaining procedures

Nebraska

Name of Court: County Court

Dollar Limitation: $1,500 (exclusive of interest and costs)

Interest Rate on Judgments: Rate is that provided by contract (maximum of 16%). If no contract, then rate determined by price of U.S. Treasury bills.

Attorneys Allowed: No

Statutory Filing Fee: $5 (Note: This fee may not include all costs involved in the individual county's filing fee. Additional fees for court automation, library, security, etc., are allowed.)

Statute of Limitation:

Most Contract Actions: 5 Years for written, 4 Years for oral
Most Tort Actions: 1-2 Years
Judgments: 5 Years
Lien on real estate: 5 Years
Renewable: Yes; within ten years after 5 year lien period, by motion and order of court. Must notice other party.

Methods of Service of Process:

Individual

1. Certified mail

2. Sheriff

3. Person authorized by law

4. Person not a party, appointed by court

Corporation

Must serve registered agent

To obtain corporation information:

Secretary of State
(402) 471-2554

Wage Garnishment Exemptions: Lesser of 25% of disposable earnings, amount by which disposable earnings exceed 30 times federal minimum hourly wage, or 15% of disposable earnings if head of household.

Homestead Exemption: $10,000 value limitation, and 2 lots in city or 160 acres in country—area limitation.

Personal Property Exemptions:

1. Wearing apparel

2. Household furnishings, up to $1,500 value

3. Equipment and tools, up to $1,500 value

4. Fuel for six months

5. In lieu of homestead, personal property to be selected by debtor, up to $2,500

6. Insurance policies, $5,000 loan value, full value if payable at death

7. Burial plots

Judgment Lien on Real Estate: A judgment is not an automatic lien if entered in small claims court. A transcript of the judgment must be filed in the office of the clerk of the district court of the county in which the defendant owns property to have a properly filed lien.

Nevada

Name of Court: Justice's Court For Small Claims

Dollar Limitation: $2,500 (exclusive of interest and costs)

Interest Rate on Judgments: Amount specified in contract

Attorneys Allowed: Yes

Filing Fee: $15 for claims between $1-$1,500, $25 for claims $501-$1,500, $35 for claims $1,501-$2,500

Statute of Limitation:

Most Contract Actions: 4 Years for oral, 6 Years for written
Most Tort Actions: 2 Years
Judgments: 6 Years

Methods of Service of Process:

Individual

1. Sheriff or his Deputy

2. Any citizen of the United States over 18 years of age

Corporation

Must serve registered agent

To obtain corporation information:

Secretary of State
(702) 687-5105

Wage Garnishment Exemptions: Lesser of 25% of disposable earnings, or amount by which disposable earnings exceed 30 times federal minimum hourly wage.

Homestead Exemption: $95,000 equity in a residence

Personal Property Exemptions:

1. Library, family pictures and keepsakes, up to $1,500 value

2. Household furnishings, up to $3,000 value

3. Farm equipment, up to $4,500 value

4. Professional libraries, tools of trade, up to $4,500

5. One motor vehicle, up to $1,000

Judgment Lien on Real Estate: A judgment is not an automatic lien on debtor's real estate. A certified copy of the judgment must be filed with the county clerk in each county where the debtor owns property to have a properly filed lien.

New Hampshire

Name of Court: Small Claims Court

Dollar Limitation: $2,500 (exclusive of interest and costs)

Interest Rate on Judgments: 10% or amount specified in contract

Statutory Filing Fee: $10 for the first defendant, $5 for each additional defendant (Note: This fee may not include all costs involved in the individual county's filing fee. Additional fees for court automation, library, security, etc., are allowed.)

Statute of Limitation:

Most Contract Actions: 4 Years for contract sale of goods
Most Tort Actions: Varies depending on action
Judgments: 20 Years, 6 Years lien on real estate

Methods of Service of Process:

Individual

1. Registered mail

2. Sheriff or Deputy

Corporation

Must serve registered agent

To obtain corporation information:

Secretary of State
(603) 271-3216

Wage Garnishment Exemptions: Fifty times the federal minimum hourly wage is exempt.

Homestead Exemption: $5,000 equity in a residence

Personal Property Exemptions:

1. Wearing apparel

2. Household goods and furniture, up to $2,000 value

3. Stove and refrigerator

4. Sewing machine

5. Fuel, up to $400 value

6. Family books, up to $800 value

7. Tools of trade, up to $1,200

8. Some farm animals

9. Pew in church

10. Cemetery plot

11. Motor vehicle, up to $1,000 value

12. Jewelry, up to $500 value

Judgment Lien on Real Estate: A judgment is not an automatic lien if entered in small claims court. A transcript of the judgment must be filed in the office of the clerk of the district court of the county in which the defendant owns property to have a properly filed lien.

Attorney Referral Service: (603) 224-6934

New Jersey

Name of Court: Superior Court, Special Civil Division

Dollar Limitation: $5,000 (exclusive of interest and costs)

Interest Rate on Judgments: 6% or amount specified in contract

Statutory Filing Fee: $12 (Note: This fee may not include all costs involved in the individual county's filing fee. Additional fees for court automation, library, security, etc., are allowed.)

Statute of Limitation:

Most Contract Actions: Some 16 Years, some 6 Years, 4 Years for contract for sale of goods
Most Tort Actions: Some 6 Years, some 2 Years
Judgments: 20 Years
Lien on Real Estate: 20 Years

Methods of Service of Process:

Individual

1. Sheriff

2. Sergeant-at-arms

3. Person specially appointed by court

Corporation

Must serve registered agent

To obtain corporation information:

Secretary of State
(609) 530-6400

Wage Garnishment Rules: Can only garnish when wages are at least $48 per week. 10% can be garnished on income of $7,500 or less per year. Higher percentage if higher income, percentage to be determined by court.

Homestead Exemption: No statutory exemption, but debtor who is in possession of residence with spouse creates a right of joint possession.

Personal Property Exemptions:

1. Wearing apparel

2. All other personal property, up to $1,000 value—debtor may select

3. Certain benefits and insurance payments

Judgment Lien on Real Estate: A judgment is an automatic lien on debtor's real estate within the county in which the judgment was received.

New Mexico

Name of Court: Magistrate Court, Small Claims Division

Dollar Limitation: $5,000 (exclusive of interest and costs)

Interest Rate on Judgments: 15% or amount specified in contract

Statutory Filing Fee: $30

Statute of Limitation:

Most Contract Actions: 6 Years for written contracts, 4 Years for oral contracts, 4 Years for sale of goods under UCC
Most Tort Actions: 3 Years
Judgments: 14 Years
Judgment Liens on Real Estate: 14 Years

Methods of Service of Process:

Individual

1. Sheriff

2. Any other person, not a party to the action, over 18 years of age

Corporation

Must serve registered agent

To obtain corporation information:

Secretary of State
(505) 827-4504

Wage Garnishment Rules: Plaintiff must leave a bond with the court in double the amount claimed in the complaint to protect a defendant from being wrongfully garnished.

Wage Garnishment Exemptions: Lesser of 25% of disposable earnings, or amount disposable earnings exceed 40 times federal minimum hourly wage.

Homestead Exemption: $20,000 equity in a residence. If joint owners, each owner allowed $20,000 equity in a residence.

Personal Property Exemptions:

1. Personal property, up to $500 value

2. Motor vehicle, up to $4,000 value

3. Wearing apparel

4. Household furnishings

5. Tools of trade, up to $1,500 value

6. Family books

7. Heath aids

8. Jewelry, up to $2,500 value

9. Pension plans and retirement funds

Judgment Lien on Real Estate: A judgment is not an automatic lien on debtor's real estate. A certified copy of the judgment must be filed with the county clerk in each county where the debtor owns property.

New York

Name of Court: Small Claims Court

Dollar Limitation: $2,000 (exclusive of interest and costs) (May vary depending on whether court is upstate or downstate)

Interest Rate on Judgments: 9%

Statutory Filing Fee: $35(Note: This fee may not include all costs involved in the individual county's filing fee. Additional fees for court automation, library, security, etc., are allowed.)

Statute of Limitation:

Most Contract Actions: 6 Years, 4 Years for contract for sale of goods
Most Tort Actions: 3 Years
Judgments: 10 Years
Lien on Real Estate: 10 Years
Renewable: Yes, for 10 years.

Methods of Service of Process:

Individual

1. Sheriff or town Marshall

2. Private Process Server

Corporation

Must serve registered agent, officer of corporation or secretary of state

To obtain corporation information:

Secretary of State
(518) 474-4750

Wage Garnishment Exemptions: If a judgement debtor receives more than $85 per week, a garnishment may be brought against the debtor for 10% of wages.

Homestead Exemption: $10,000 equity in a residence.

Personal Property Exemptions:

1. Certain life and disability insurance benefits

2. Unemployment

3. Worker's compensation

4. Certain pensions

5. Welfare

6. Burial plot

7. Stove, sewing machine

8. Family Bible, pictures and school books

9. Other books, up to $50 value

10. Domestic animals, up to $450 value

11. Wearing apparel, household furnishings

12. Tools of the trade, up to $600 value

Judgment Lien on Real Estate: A judgment is not an automatic lien on debtor's real estate within the county. A cerified copy of the judgment must be filed with the county clerk in each county where the debtor owns property, to have a properly filed lien in that county.

Note:

1. Hearing set 15-30 days from filing date.

2. Court may order judgment amount to be paid into the court by a certain date.

3. Be aware that many of the rules vary depending on the location of the court. New York City and Buffalo courts vary greatly.

North Carolina

Name of Court: Small Claims Court

Dollar Limitation: $2,000 (exclusive of interest and costs)

Interest Rate on Judgments: 8% or amount specified in contract

Statutory Filing Fee: $30

Statute of Limitation:

> Most Contract Actions: 3 Years
> Most Tort Actions: 1-2 Years
> Judgments: 10 Years
> Lien on Real Estate: 10 Years

Methods of Service of Process:

> *Individual*
>
> 1. Sheriff
>
> 2. Any other person authorized to serve summons
>
> *Corporation*
>
> Must serve registered agent
>
> To obtain corporation information:
>
> > Secretary of State
> > (919) 733-4201

Wage Garnishment Exemptions: Wages are exempt when by debtor's affidavit, it is apparent that the earnings are necessary for debtor's family's use.

Homestead Exemption: Set by state legislature—no less than $1,000 equity in a residence.

Personal Property Exemptions: Personal property determined by legislature—no less than $500 to be selected by debtor.

Judgment Lien on Real Estate: A judgment is an automatic lien on debtor's real estate.

Attorney Referral Service: (800) 662-7660 or (919) 828-1054

North Dakota

Name of Court: Small Claims Court of County Court

Dollar Limitation: $2,000 (exclusive of interest and costs)

Interest Rate on Judgments: 12% or amount specified in contract

Statutory Filing Fee: $10 (Note: This fee may not include all costs involved in the individual county's filing fee. Additional fees for court automation, library, security, etc., are allowed.)

Statute of Limitation:

Most Contract Actions: 6 Years for oral or written
Most Tort Actions: 2 Years
Judgments: 10 Years

Methods of Service of Process:

Individual

1. Any person of legal age not a party

Corporation

Must serve registered agent

To obtain corporation information:

Secretary of State
(701) 224-2900

Wage Garnishment Rules: No garnishment or attachment is allowed through small claims court.

Wage Garnishment Exemptions: Lesser of 25% of disposable earnings, or amount by which disposable earnings exceed 40 times federal minimum hourly wage.

Homestead Exemption: $80,000 equity in a residence.

Personal Property Exemptions:

1. Household goods

2. Furnishings and other personal property, up to $5,000 value

Judgment Lien on Real Estate: A judgment is not an automatic lien on debtor's real estate. A certified copy of the judgment must be filed with the county clerk in each county where the debtor owns property to have a properly filed lien in that county.

Ohio

Name of Court: Small Claims Court

Dollar Limitation: $1,000 (exclusive of interest and costs)

Interest Rate on Judgements: 8%

Attorneys Allowed: Yes

Statutory Filing Fee: Various, not to exceed 1/2 of filing fee charged in general court. (Note: This fee may not include all costs involved in the individual county's filing fee. Additional fees for court automation, library, security, etc., are allowed.)

Statute of Limitation:

Most Contract Actions: 15 Years for written contract, 6 Years for oral contract, 4 Years for contract for sale of goods (UCC)
Most Tort Actions: 2 Years

Methods of Service of Process:

Individual

1. Sheriff

2. Person appointed by court over 18 years of age and not a party

Corporation

Must serve registered agent

To obtain corporation information:

Secretary of State
(614) 466-3910

Wage Garnishment Rules: Demand letter must be sent either by personal service or certified mail 15-45 days before garnishment.

Wage Garnishment Exemptions: If paid weekly, 30 times federal minimum hourly wage; biweekly, 60 times federal minimum hourly wage; semimonthly, 65 times federal minimum hourly wage; monthly, 130 times federal minimum hourly wage.

Homestead Exemption: $5,000 equity in a residence.

Personal Property Exemptions:

1. Motor vehicle, up to $1,000 value

2. Wearing apparel and bedding, up to $200 value

3. Stove and refrigerator, up to $300 value

4. Additional household furnishings, up to $200 value

5. Jewelry, up to $600 value

6. Additional personal items if no homestead exemption is claimed, up to $2,000 value; if homestead exemption is claimed, up to $1,500 value

7. Tools of trade or books, up to $750 value

8. Health aids

9. Burial plot

10. Worker's Compensation, unemployment, insurance benefits, and retirement benefits

11. Alimony and child support

Judgment Lien on Real Estate: A judgment is not an automatic lien on debtor's real estate. A certified copy of the judgment must be filed with the county clerk in each county where the debtor owns property to have a properly filed lien in that county.

Oklahoma

Name of Court: Small Claims Court of the District Court

Dollar Limitation: $2,500 (exclusive of interest and costs)

Interest Rate on Judgments: Amount contract specified or amount figured from Treasury Bill rate for preceding year

Attorneys Allowed: Yes

Filing Fee: $37 for claims $1-$1,500, $64 for claims $1,501-$2,500

Statute of Limitation:

Most Contract Actions: 5 Years for written, 3 Years for oral
Most Tort Actions: 1-2 Years

Methods of Service of Process:

Individual

1. Certified mail, return receipt requested

2. Sheriff

3. Licensed private process server

4. Person specially appointed by the court

Corporation

Must serve registered agent

To obtain corporation information:

Secretary of State
(918) 820-2424

Wage Garnishment Exemptions: 75% of earnings is exempt.

Homestead Exemption: Rural—160 acres; City—acre or $5,000 value, whichever is more.

Personal Property Exemptions:

1. Certain disability, retirement and insurance benefits

2. Furniture

3. Cemetery plot

4. Tools of trade

5. Family books and pictures

6. Wearing apparel, up to $4,000 value

7. Motor vehicle, up to $3,000 value

8. Certain farm animals

9. Alimony and support payments

10. Worker's compensation

Judgment Lien on Real Estate: A judgment is not an automatic lien on debtor's real estate. A certified copy of the judgment must be filed with the county clerk in each county where the debtor owns property, if applicable.

Oregon

Name of Court: District Court, Small Claims Division

Dollar Limitation: $2,500 (exclusive of interest and costs)

Interest Rate on Judgments: 9% or amount specified in contract

Attorneys Allowed: Not without consent of court

Filing Fee: $34.10 for claims $1-$1,500, $67.90 for claims $1,501-$2,500

Statute of Limitation:

Most Contract Actions: 6 Years, 4 Years for contract for sale of goods
Most Tort Actions: 2 Years
Judgments: 10 Years

Methods of Service of Process:

Individual

1. Certified mail

2. Any competent, disinterested person at least 18 years of age

Corporation

Must serve registered agent

To obtain corporation information:

Secretary of State
(503) 378-4166

Wage Garnishment Exemptions: Lesser of 25% of disposable earnings, or amount by which disposable earnings exceed 40 times federal minimum hourly wage.

Homestead Exemption: $15,000 equity in a residence for 1 debtor; $20,000 equity in a residence for 2 or more debtors in same house.

Personal Property Exemptions:

1. Books, pictures and musical instruments, up to $300 value

2. Wearing apparel and jewelry, up to $900 value

3. Tools of trade, up to $750 value

4. Motor vehicle, up to $1,200 value

5. Animals for family use, up to $1,000 value

6. Household furnishings, up to $1,450 value

7. Heath aid and child support

8. Maintenance

9. Payment for personal injury up to $7,500

10. Certain pensions, benefits, social security

11. Burial plot

Judgment Lien on Real Estate: A judgment from a small claims court is not a lien until certified copy is filed with circuit court.

Pennsylvania

Name of Court: Magistrate Court

Dollar Limitation: $2,000 (exclusive of interest and costs)

Interest Rate on Judgments: 6%

Attorneys Allowed: Yes

Filing Fee: If claim is below $100—$16.50; if claim is above $100 but not more than $300—$21.50; if claim is above $300 but not more than $500—$34.00; if claim is above $500 but not more than $2000—$39.00. (Note: This fee may not include all costs involved in the individual county's filing fee. Additional fees for court automation, library, security, etc., are allowed.)

Statute of Limitation:

Most Contract Actions: 4 Years for contract for sale of goods, 4 Years for oral, 4 Years for written
Most Tort Actions: 1-2 Years
Judgments: 4 Years

Methods of Service of Process:

Individual

1. Sheriff or coroner if sheriff is a party

Corporation

Must serve registered agent. If registered agent not listed, serve anyone at registered address.

To obtain corporation information:

Secretary of State
(717) 787-1057

Wage Garnishment Exemptions: All wages are exempt

Homestead Exemption: No homestead law

Personal Property Exemptions:

1. Wearing apparel and certain uniforms

2. Family books

3. Sewing machine

4. Certain retirement and insurance benefits

5. Other personal property, up to a $300 value

Judgment Lien on Real Estate: A judgment is an automatic lien on real estate of the debtor's within the county in which the judgment was received.

Rhode Island

Name of Court: Small Claims Court of the District Court

Dollar Limitation: $1,500 (exclusive of interest and costs)

Interest Rate on Judgments: 12% unless based on the contract, then goes by contract rate

Attorneys Allowed: Yes

Statutory Filing Fee: $5 (Note: This fee may not include all costs involved in the individual county's filing fee. Additional fees for court automation, library, security, etc., are allowed.)

Statute of Limitation:

Most Contract Actions: Some 10 Years and some 20 Years
Most Tort Actions: 3 Years
Judgments: 20 Years

Methods of Service of Process:

Individual

1. Registered mail

2. Certified mail

3. Sheriff or Deputy Sheriff

4. Town sergeant

5. Constable

6. As otherwise provided by the court

Corporation

Must serve registered agent

To obtain corporation information:

Secretary of State
(401) 277-2357

Wage Garnishment Exemptions: Wages up to $50 are absolutely exempt.

Homestead Exemption: No homestead exemption.

Personal Property Exemptions:

1. Wearing apparel

2. Tools of trade, up to $500 value

3. Professional library of professional person

4. Household furnishings, up to $1,000 value

5. Accident or disability benefits

6. Life insurance benefits

Judgment Lien on Real Estate: A judgment is not an automatic lien on debtor's real estate. A certified copy of the judgment must be filed with the county clerk in each county where the debtor owns property.

South Carolina

Name of Court: Magistrate's Court

Dollar Limitation: $2,500 (exclusive of interest and costs)

Interest Rate on Judgments: 14%

Attorneys Allowed: Yes

Statutory Filing Fee: $35 (Note: This fee may not include all costs involved in the individual county's filing fee. Additional fees for court automation, library, security, etc., are allowed.)

Statute of Limitation:

Most Contract Actions: 3 Years
Most Tort Actions: 2-3 Years
Judgments: 10 Years on lien on real estate

Methods of Service of Process:

Individual

1. Sheriff or Deputy

2. Person over 18 years of age not attorney or a party to the action

Corporation

Must serve registered agent

To obtain corporation information:

Secretary of State
P.O. Box 11350
Columbia, SC 29211
(803) 734-2158

Wage Garnishment Exemptions: All wages exempt

Homestead Exemption: One residence

Judgment Lien on Real Estate: A judgment is not an automatic lien on debtor's real estate. A certified copy of the judgment must be file owns property.

South Carolina Law Line Service: (800) 521-9788 or (803) 771-0011

Note: A pamphlet on civil proceedings in the Magistrate's Court is available from the clerk.

South Dakota

Name of Court: Small Claims Court

Dollar Limitation: $2,000 (exclusive of interest and costs)

Interest Rate on Judgments: 12%

Attorneys Allowed: $2,000

Statutory Filing Fee: $4 for claims under $100; $10 for claims under $1,000; $20 for claims over $1,000. (Note: This fee may not include all costs involved in the individual county's filing fee. Additional fees for court automation, library, security, etc., are allowed.)

Statute of Limitation:

Most Contract Actions: 4 Years for contract for sale of goods—UCC, 6 Years for written
Most Tort Actions: 2-3 Years
Judgments: 20 Years, 10 Years on lien on real estate

Methods of Service of Process:

Individual

1. Certified mail

2. Sheriff or constable

3. Any person not a party to the action who is an elector of county in which service is made

Corporation

Must serve registered agent

To obtain corporation information:

Secretary of State
(605) 773-3537
(605) 773-4845

Wage Garnishment Exemptions: Lesser of 20% of disposable earnings for the week or 40 times federal minimum wage, whichever is greater exemption.

Homestead Exemption: $30,000 value—1 acre in town or 160 acres in country. Unlimited for debtor 70 years of age or older.

Personal Property Exemptions:

1. All family pictures

2. A church pew

3. Burial plot

4. Family library, up to $200 value

5. Wearing apparel

6. Fuel for 1 year

7. Additional exemptions, up to $4,000 value if head of household, or $2,000 if single and not head of household

8. Certain health and life insurance benefits

Judgment Lien on Real Estate: A judgment is an automatic lien on all property in county except homestead land.

Note: Court may order judgment paid at a certain time or in installments.

Tennessee

Name of Court: Courts of General Session

Dollar Limitation: $10,000, $15,000 in Shelby county (exclusive of interest and costs)

Interest Rate on Judgments: 10% of amount specified in contract

Attorneys Allowed: Yes

Statutory Filing Fee: $48.75

Statute of Limitation:

Most Contract Actions: 6 Years for written and oral, 4 Years for contract for sale of goods
Most Tort Actions: 1 Year
Judgments: 10 Years

Methods of Service of Process:

Individual

1. Sheriff or Deputy

2. Process server appointed by court

3. Certified mail, return receipt requested

4. Registered mail

Corporation

Must serve registered agent

To obtain corporation information:

Department of State, Division of Svcs.
Attn: Certifications
Suite 1800
James K. Polk Building
Nashville, TN 37243-0306
(615) 741-2286

Cost is $10.00 per corporate inquiry.

Wage Garnishment Rules: No garnishment shall be released except as authorized by judge or clerk. All monies received through garnishment shall be paid to the clerk of the court.

Wage Garnishment Exemptions: Lesser of 25% of disposable earnings, or amount by which disposable earnings exceed 30 times federal minimum hourly wage.

Homestead Exemption: $5,000 equity in a residence.

Personal Property Exemptions:

1. Wearing apparel

2. Family pictures and books

3. Additional personal property, up to $4,000 value

4. Accident, health and disability insurance benefits

5. Certain pensions, social security and unemployment benefits

6. Tools of trade, up to $750 value

7. Alimony

Judgment Lien on Real Estate: A judgment is not an automatic lien on debtor's real estate. A certified copy of the judgment must be filed with the county clerk in each county where the debtor owns property.

Texas

Name of Court: Small Claims Court

Dollar Limitation: Varies up to $5,000 depending on county (exclusive of interest and costs)

Interest Rate on Judgments: 18% or amount specified in the contract

Attorneys Allowed: Yes

Statutory Filing Fee: $10

Statute of Limitation:

Most Contract Actions: 4 Years
Most Tort Actions: 2 Years
Judgments: 10 Years

Methods of Service of Process:

Individual

1. Sheriff or constable

2. Person 18 years of age or older not a party to the action by written order of the court

Corporation

Must serve registered agent

To obtain corporation information:

Secretary of State
(512) 463-5555

Wage Garnishment Rules: Not allowed

Wage Garnishment Exemptions: All wages are exempt

Homestead Exemption: 200 acres for family, 100 acres for single debtor in rural area, 1 acre in city.

Personal Property Exemptions:

1. Household furnishings

2. Farming equipment or other tools of trade

3. Two firearms

4. Numerous farm animals

5. Cash surrender value of life insurance policy

6. Two motor vehicles

7. Certain IRA accounts

8. Limitation of personal property exemption ($15,000 for single person, $30,000 for family)

Judgment Lien on Real Estate: A judgment is not an automatic lien on debtor's real estate. A certified copy of the judgment must be filed with the county clerk in each county where the debtor owns property.

Utah

Name of Court: Small Claims Department of Circuit Court

Dollar Limitation: $1,000 (exclusive of interest and costs)

Interest Rate on Judgements: 12% or amount specified in contract

Statutory Filing Fee: $15 (Note: This fee may not include all costs involved in the individual county's filing fee. Additional fees for court automation, library, security, etc., are allowed.)

Statute of Limitation:

Most Contract Actions: 6 Years for written, 4 Years for oral contract
Most Tort Actions: Some 1, some 2, some 4 Years
Judgments: 8 Years

Methods of Service of Process:

Individual

1. Anyone over 21 years of age, not a party to action

2. Sheriff

Note: Defendant's appearance date is 4-45 days from date of order

Corporation

Must serve registered agent

To obtain corporation information:

Secretary of State
(801) 530-4849

Wage Garnishment Exemptions: Lesser of 25% of disposable earnings, or amount by which disposable earnings exceed 30 times federal minimum hourly wage.

Homestead Exemption: $8,000 equity in a residence for head of household, $2,000 equity in a residence for spouse, $500 equity in a residence per dependent.

Judgment Lien on Real Estate: A judgment is an automatic lien on debtor's real estate within county where sued. Other counties require a certified copy of judgment filed with clerk of district court.

Vermont

Name of Court: Small Claims Court

Dollar Limitation: $2,000 (exclusive of interest and costs)

Interest Rate on Judgments: 12%

Statutory Filing Fee: $25 for claims $500 or less, $35 for claims more than $500 (Note: This fee may not include all costs involved in the individual county's filing fee. Additional fees for court automation, library, security, etc., are allowed.)

Statute of Limitation:

Most Contract Actions: 6-8 Years, 4 Years for contract for sale of goods
Most Tort Actions: 3 Years
Judgments: 8 Years

Methods of Service of Process:

Individual

1. Registered mail

2. Sheriff or deputy sheriff

3. Constable

4. Person specially appointed

Corporation

Must serve registered agent

To obtain corporation information:

Secretary of State
(802) 828-2363

Wage Garnishment Exemptions: Lesser of 25% of disposable earnings, or amount by which disposable earnings exceed 30 times federal minimum hourly wage. If the judgment is for a consumer credit transaction, the exemption is lesser of 15% of disposable earnings, or amount by which disposable earnings exceed 40 times federal minimum hourly wage.

Homestead Exemption: $30,000 equity in a residence

Personal Property Exemptions:

1. Wearing apparel, bedding, tools, arms, and household furniture necessary for sustaining life

2. Sewing machine

3. Family books

4. Professional books and instruments up to $200

5. Social Security and SSI

6. Various benefits, including veteran's, unemployment, pension, worker's compensation, welfare, public assistance

7. Insurance payments

Judgment Lien on Real Estate: A judgment is not an automatic lien on debtor's real estate. A certified copy of the judgment must be filed with the county clerk in each county where the debtor owns property.

Virginia

Name of Court: Small Claims Court in Fairfax and Arlington Counties. Otherwise, claims are handled under circuit court.

Dollar Limitation: $1,000 (exclusive of interest and costs)

Interest Rate on Judgments: 8% or amount specified in contract

Attorneys Allowed: Not typically

Statutory Filing Fee: $15 for claims of $500 and below, $25 for claims of $500 to $1,000. (Note: This fee may not include all costs involved in the individual county's filing fee. Additional fees for court automation, library, security, etc., are allowed.)

Statute of Limitation:

Most Contract Actions: 5 Years for written, 4 Years for contract for sale of goods
Most Tort Actions: 2 Years
Judgments: 20 Years
Renewable: Yes

Methods of Service of Process:

Individual

1. Officer

2. Any disinterested person

Corporation

Must serve registered agent

To obtain corporation information:

State Corporation Commission
(804) 786-3733

Wage Garnishment Exemptions: Lesser of 25% of disposable earnings, or amount by which disposable earnings exceed 30 times federal minimum hourly wage.

Homestead Exemption: $5,000 equity in a residence

Personal Property Exemptions:

1. Certain pensions, benefits and insurance payments

2. Family Bible

3. Wedding and engagement rings

4. Family portraits, heirlooms, up to $5,000 value

5. Burial plot

6. One motor vehicle, up to $2,000 value

7. Wearing apparel, up to $1,000 value

8. Necessary health aids

9. Tools of trade, up to $10,000 value

Judgment Lien on Real Estate: A judgment is not an automatic lien on debtor's real estate. A certified copy of the judgment must be filed with the county clerk in each county where the debtor owns property.

Washington

Name of Court: District court

Dollar Limitation: $2,000 (exclusive of interest and costs)

Interest Rate on Judgements: 12% or amount specified in contract

Attorneys Allowed: No

Statutory Filing Fee: $10 (Note: This fee may not include all costs involved in the individual county's filing fee. Additional fees for court automation, library, security, etc., are allowed.)

Statute of Limitation:

Most Contract Actions: 6 Years, 4 Years for contract sale of goods
Most Tort Actions: 2 Years
Judgments: 10 Years on real estate lien

Methods of Service of Process:

Individual

1. Sheriff or Deputy

2. Any person over 18 years of age not a party to action

Corporation

Must serve registered agent

To obtain corporation information:

Secretary of State
(206) 753-7115

Wage Garnishment Exemptions: Lesser of 25% of disposable earnings, or amount by which disposable earnings exceed 30 times federal minimum hourly wage.

Homestead Exemption: $30,000 equity in a residence

Personal Property Exemptions:

1. Wearing apparel, up to $750 value

2. Family pictures and books, up to $1,000 value

3. Household furnishings, up to $1,500 value

4. 3 months of fuel

5. Other personal property, up to $500 value

6. Motor vehicle, up to $1,200 value

7. Farming equipment or other tools of trade, up to $3,000 value

8. Some pensions and insurance benefits

Judgment Lien on Real Estate: If judgment is not paid within 20 days of time specified by court, it is automatically entered as a lien on defendant's property within county.

West Virginia

Name of Court: County Magistrates' Court

Dollar Limitation: $3,000 (exclusive of interest and costs)

Interest Rate on Judgments: 10%

Attorneys Allowed: Yes

Statutory Filing Fee: $20 for claims $1-$500, $25 for claims $501-$1,000, $30 for claims $1,001-$1,500, $40 for claims $1,501-$3,000

Statute of Limitation:

Most Contract Actions: 5 Years, 4 Years for contract for sale of goods
Most Tort Actions: 2 Years
Judgments: 10 Years on lien on real estate
Renewable: Yes

Methods of Service of Process:

Individual

1. Sheriff

2. Any person of age not a party to the action except for attorneys to the parties

Corporation

Must serve registered agent

To obtain corporation information:

Secretary of State
(304) 345-4000
(304) 342-8000

Wage Garnishment Exemptions: Lesser of 20% of disposable earnings or amount by which disposable earnings exceed 30 times federal minimum hourly wage.

Homestead Exemption: $5,000 equity in a residence

Personal Property Exemptions:

1. Personal property, up to $1,000 value

2. Tools of trade, up to $50 value

3. Life insurance cash surrender value

4. Certain benefits

5. Worker's Compensation payments and pension payments

Judgment Lien on Real Estate: A judgment is not an automatic lien on debtor's real estate. A certified copy of the judgment must be filed with the county clerk in each county where the debtor owns property.

Wisconsin

Name of Court: Small Claims Court

Dollar Limitation: $2,000 (exclusive of interest and costs)

Interest Rate on Judgments: 12%

Attorneys Allowed: Yes

Statutory Filing Fee: $22 (Note: This fee may not include all costs involved in the individual county's filing fee. Additional fees for court automation, library, security, etc., are allowed.)

Methods of Service of Process:

Individual

1. Service by certified mail if defendant lives within county case is being filed in

2. Any adult resident not a party to the action

Corporation

Must serve registered agent

To obtain corporation information:

Secretary of State
(608) 266-3590

Wage Garnishment Exemptions: Lesser of 25% of disposable earnings, or amount by which disposable earnings exceed 30 times federal minimum hourly wage.

Homestead Exemption: $40,000 equity in a residence, but may not exceed 40 acres.

Personal Property Exemptions:

1. Personal property, up to $5,000 value

2. Business and farm property, up to $7,500 value

3. Certain proceeds of life insurance

4. Disability benefits

5. Pensions

6. Personal injury awards

Judgment Lien on Real Estate: A judgment is not an automatic lien on debtor's real estate. A certified copy of the judgment must be filed with the county clerk in each county where the debtor owns property.

Lawyer Referral and Information Service: (800) 362-9082

Wyoming

Name of Court: County Court, Small Claims Division

Dollar Limitation: $2,000 (exclusive of interest and costs)

Interest Rate on Judgments: 10% or amount specified in contract

Statutory Filing Fee: $4 (Note: This fee may not include all costs involved in the individual county's filing fee. Additional fees for court automation, library, security, etc., are allowed.)

Statute of Limitation:

Most Contract Actions: 10 Years for written, 8 Years for oral
Most Tort Actions: 1, 2, or 4 Years

Methods of Service of Process:

Individual

1. Registered mail, return receipt requested

2. Sheriff or Deputy

3. Any person 21 years of age or older not a party appointed by the clerk

Note: Defendant must appear informally in court 3-12 days after service of summons.

Corporation

Must serve registered agent

To obtain corporation information:

Secretary of State
(307) 777-7378

Wage Garnishment Rules: Attachment and garnishment are not allowed in small claims court.

Wage Garnishment Exemptions: All wages are exempt

Homestead Exemption: $10,000 equity in a residence

Personal Property Exemptions:

1. Family books and pictures

2. Burial plot

3. Household furnishings, up to $2,000 value

4. Motor vehicle, up to $2,000 value

5. Wearing apparel, including wedding rings, up to $1,000 value

6. Certain retirement benefits

7. Tools of trade, up to $2,000 value

8. Life insurance proceeds, disability, and insurance benefits

Judgment Lien on Real Estate: A judgment is an automatic lien on debtor's real estate. Must demand payment and be refused before you can file a complaint.

Appendix A

Sample Letters and Forms

First Demand Letter—
Business v. Debtor

August 30, 199_

Darlene E. Debtor
5th Street
Hurst, IL 62949

Re: Account #7645032

Dear Ms. Debtor,

Thank you for doing business with our office. We are appreciative of your business and would hope to continue our working relationship. Our records however show that you are 30 days late in paying on your account. We know that this is probably an oversight and that you intend to pay this as soon as possible. Please consider this to be a friendly reminder.

Sincerely,

Mr./Ms. Businessperson

First Demand Letter—
Individual v. Business

August 30, 199_

The Michael Cale Repair Company
5th Street
Hurst, IL 62949

Re: Repairs done August 15, 199_ at 101 4th St., Hurst, IL

Dear Mr. Cale,

Thank you for the prompt service in repairing the leaky pipes in the kitchen. However, it appears that because of incorrect patching of the pipes, the problem has multiplied, with leaks springing up all over the house. I have contacted your office numerous times and have gotten no satisfaction as to a solution. If I do not have these pipes fixed by your company by September 5, 199_ , I will be forced to contact another repair company and hold you responsible for the charges.

Please let me know what your intentions are in this matter.

Sincerely,

Mr./Ms. Homeowner

Payment Plan Letter

June 3, 199_

Ms. Barbara Stanley
P.O. Box 5
Oreana, AL 42112

Dear Ms. Stanley,

Thank you for your payment plan offer on the $2,000 bill which you owe. As agreed, I am willing to accept $400 payments per month for 5 months until this debt is satisfied. The payments are due on the 15th of each month, beginning June 15, 199_ and continuing monthly through October 15th, 199_.

As agreed, as long as the payments are made in a timely fashion, I will withhold all further action.

Thank you for your cooperation in this matter.

Sincerely,

Lisa Leroy

Delinquent Payments

Bill Anderson
213 Trout River Boulevard
Jackson, WI 54212

Re: Account #7563042

Dear Mr. Anderson,

On June 3, 199_, we agreed to a monthly payment arrangement of $400. Although the first payment was made on June 15, 199_, we have not received the following two payments. We are anxious to work with you in this matter to bring you up to date on your obligation. Please contact the office immediately or send in the delinquent balance.

If we do not hear from you in the next 5 days, we will be forced to collect this debt through legal avenues. I look forward to hearing from you and clearing up the delinquent balance.

Sincerely,

Fern Beitz
Beitz Dairy Products

Settlement Letter

April 4, 199_

Mr. Donald Debtor
132 W. Main
Colfax, CA 90066

Re: Your account #7234671

Dear Mr. Debtor,

As orally agreed, my company is willing to accept $520 as a full and complete settlement of your account.

This sum must be paid by April 21, 199_ or this offer will become void.

Thank you for working with us on this matter.

Sincerely,

Tom Egert
Egert Enterprises

Final Demand Letter—
Business v. Debtor (Individual)

August 5, 199_

Randy N. Debtor
5th Street
Carbondale, IL 62901

Re: Account #7532814

Dear Mr. Debtor,

Your immediate attention in paying the debt owed in the amount of $100.00 for telephone repair services is necessary to avoid further action being taken against you.

If you do not make payment in full by August 19, 199_, a lawsuit will be filed against you. A hearing date will be set and you will be notified by summons at your residence or place of employment. If you do not pay the amount due prior to the hearing date and do not appear for the hearing, a default judgment will be entered against you. A judgment will be a lien against your property and will be a record on your credit report. If you do appear for the purpose of contesting the bill, a trial date will be set.

(the following is optional)

It is our policy not to accept installment payments on the debt. However, in some cases exceptions are made. I am enclosing an affidavit which you may complete and return to me. You may make an offer of installment payments in the space provided near the bottom of the page. This statement will not be accepted unless it is signed under oath before a notary public.

Please let me know your intentions as to this matter by August 10, 199_.

Sincerely,

Mr./Ms. Businessperson

Final Demand Letter—
Individual v. Business

September 6, 199_

The Michael Cale Repair Company
5th Street
Hurst, IL 62949

Re: Repairs done August 15, 199_ at 101 4th St., Hurst, IL

Dear Mr. Cale,

Because I have not heard from you as to your plans for fixing
the leaky pipes in my home, I was forced to hire Do-It-Right
Repair Shop to fix the damage which your company caused. The
bill is attached and I am holding your company responsible in
this matter.

Please pay this bill by September 15, 199_ to avoid legal action.

Sincerely,

Mr./Ms. Homeowner

Small Claims Complaint—Automobile

STATE OF _____

IN THE CIRCUIT COURT OF THE _____ JUDICIAL CIRCUIT

COUNTY OF _____

_____
Plaintiff

v.   Case No. _____

_____
Defendant

COMPLAINT

NOW COMES the plaintiff, _____ and complains of the defendant, ____ _____and states as follows:

On or about _____ in the vicinity of _____ on a public highway of _____ County,_____plaintiff's motor vehicle, being operated by _____was in a collision with defendant's motor vehicle being operated by _____ with defendant's consent, and that said collision with plaintiff's vehicle was caused by the negligent and careless operation of defendant's vehicle, whereby plaintiff's vehicle was damaged and depreciated in value.

WHEREFORE Plaintiff demands judgement in the sum of $_____.

_____
Plaintiff

Plaintiff_____   Address _____

City _____   Phone _____

Small Claims Complaint—To Evict Tenant

STATE OF _____
IN THE CIRCUIT COURT OF THE _____ JUDICIAL CIRCUIT
COUNTY OF _____

_____
Plaintiff

v.   Case No. _____

_____
Defendant

COMPLAINT

NOW COMES the plaintiff, _____ and complains of the defendant, _____, and states as follows:

1.   This is an action to evict a tenant from real property in _____ County, _____.

2.   Plaintiff _____ is the agent for the owner of the following described real property in _____ County, _____:

_____

_____

3.   Defendant _____ has possession of said property under oral/written agreement to pay rent of $_____, payable _____.

4.   Defendant _____ failed to pay rent due _____.

5.   Plaintiff _____ served Defendant _____ with notice on _____ to pay said rent or deliver possession but Defendant _____ refused to do either.

WHEREFORE Plaintiff _____ demands judgement for possession of said property against Defendant.

_____
Plaintiff

Plaintiff _____   Address _____

City _____   Phone _____

Small Claims Complaint—On An Account

STATE OF _____

IN THE CIRCUIT COURT OF THE _____ JUDICIAL CIRCUIT

COUNTY OF _____

_____
Plaintiff

v.   Case No. _____

_____
Defendant

COMPLAINT

NOW COMES the plaintiff, _____
and complains of the defendant, _____
and states as follows:

1. This is an action for damages which does not exceed the sum of
_____ $(small claims limit) _____, exclusive of interest and costs.

2. There is now due, owing and unpaid from the Defendant to the
Plaintiff monies in the sum of $_____ since _____,
19_____ for: (check one)

_____ Goods sold and delivered by Plaintiff to the Defendant
according to the attached itemized statement and/or account.

_____ Work done and materials furnished by Plaintiff to
Defendant at Defendant's request, according to the attached itemized
statement and/or account.

_____ Monies due from Defendant to Plaintiff according to the
attached account.

WHEREFORE Plaintiff demands judgement in the sum of $_____
plus court costs.

_____
Plaintiff

Plaintiff _____   Address _____

City _____   Phone _____

184

Small Claims Complaint—Replevin

STATE OF _____
IN THE CIRCUIT COURT OF THE _____ JUDICIAL CIRCUIT
COUNTY OF _____

_____
            Plaintiff

        v.   Case No. _____

_____
            Defendant
                          COMPLAINT

     NOW COMES the plaintiff, _____ and complains of
the defendant, _____, and states as follows:
     1.   That the plaintiff is/are lawfully entitled to the possession of the
following described personal property, located at _____ in
_____County,_____to wit: (description of property _____
_____.

     2.   Defendant came into possession of the above said goods by virtue
of _____.

     3.   To the best of my knowledge, information and belief the value of
said property is the sum of $_____ , that said property has not
been taken for any tax, assessment or fine levied by virtue of any law of
the state of _____, nor seized under any execution or attachment against the
goods and chattels of said plaintiff liable to execution and that the above
named defendant has/have possession of the above described personal
property and wrongfully detains the same from plaintiff in the County of
_____, State of _____.

     4.   That said plaintiff is the owner of said personal property and
entitled to the possession therefore by the virtue of _____ that said defendant
_____, in _____ County, _____
wrongfully detains from said plaintiff said personal property of the value
as aforesaid; that said plaintiff made demand upon said defendant for
possession of said personal property prior to the institution of this claim,
yet said defendant continues to wrongfully withhold possession thereof
from said plaintiff_____, for reason
being_____.

     5.   Said plaintiff demands the return of said personal property and
damages for the wrongful detention thereof or for the value thereof and the
costs of this action.

                              _____
                                                    Plaintiff

Plaintiff _____   Address _____

City _____   Phone _____

Small Claims Complaint—General

STATE OF _____
IN THE CIRCUIT COURT OF THE _____ JUDICIAL CIRCUIT
COUNTY OF _____

_____
Plaintiff

v.   Case No. _____

_____
Defendant

COMPLAINT

NOW COMES the plaintiff, _____ and complains of the defendant, _____, and states as follows:

1.   That plaintiff is an individual, residing a _____
_____ .

2.   That the defendant resides at _____
_____ .

3.   That the defendant has failed to pay $ _____ to plaintiff for expenses incurred_____.

4.   These expenses include _____
_____ (See Exhibit A)

5.   That the total amount owing is $ _____ and plaintiff has requested and defendant has failed to make payment of this amount.

WHEREFORE, Plaintiff, _____ , respectfully prays that judgment be entered against defendant, _____ , for the sum of $ _____ , plus court costs.

By _____
                                                                    Plaintiff

Plaintiff _____   Address _____

City _____   Phone _____

Summons by Certified Mail

STATE OF _____
IN THE CIRCUIT COURT OF THE _____ JUDICIAL CIRCUIT
COUNTY OF _____

_____

Plaintiff

v.   Case No. _____

_____

Defendant

SUMMONS BY CERTIFIED MAIL

To each defendant:

YOU ARE SUMMONED and required to appear before this court at _____ , at _____ o'clock, ____ .m., on _____ , 19 ___ , to answer the complaint in this case, a copy of which is hereto attached. IF YOU FAIL TO DO SO, A JUDGMENT BY DEFAULT MAY BE TAKEN AGAINST YOU FOR THE RELIEF ASKED IN THE COMPLAINT.

(Seal of Court) Witness _____ , 19 _____

_____
(Clerk of the Court)

_____ , on oath says the last known mailing address of defendant _____ , is _____ .

Signed and sworn to before me _____ , 19 _____ .

_____
(Notary Public/Clerk of Court)

Plaintiff _____   City _____

Address _____   Phone _____

CERTIFICATE OF MAILING

A copy of this summons was mailed to each defendant named in the above affidavit, addressed to each at the address shown, by certified mail, return receipt requested, on _____ , 19 ____ . _____
By _____ .

(Seal of Court) By _____ , 19 _____

_____
(Clerk of the Court)

(Seal of Court) _____
(Deputy)

Summons

STATE OF _____
IN THE CIRCUIT COURT OF THE _____ JUDICIAL CIRCUIT
COUNTY OF _____

_____
      Plaintiff

    v.   Case No. _____

_____
      Defendant

SUMMONS

To each defendant:

YOU ARE SUMMONED and required to appear before this court at _____ , at _____ o'clock, _____ .m., on _____ , 19 _____ , to answer the complaint in this case, a copy of which is hereto attached. IF YOU FAIL TO DO SO, A JUDGMENT BY DEFAULT MAY BE TAKEN AGAINST YOU FOR THE RELIEF ASKED IN THE COMPLAINT.

To the officer:

This summons must be returned by the officer or other person to whom it was given for service, with indorsement of service and fees, if any, immediately after service and not less than 3 days before the day for appearance. If service cannot be made, this summons shall be returned so indorsed. This summons may not be served later than 3 days before the day for appearance.

(Seal of Court)   Witness _____ , 19 _____

_____
                 (Clerk of the Court)

Plaintiff _____   City _____

Address _____   Phone _____

Alias Summons

STATE OF _____

IN THE CIRCUIT COURT OF THE _____ JUDICIAL CIRCUIT

COUNTY OF _____

_____
      Plaintiff

     v.   Case No. _____

_____
      Defendant

ALIAS SUMMONS

To each defendant:

YOU ARE SUMMONED and required to appear before this court at _____ , at _____ o'clock, _____ .m., on _____ , 19 ____ , to answer the complaint in this case, a copy of which is hereto attached. IF YOU FAIL TO DO SO, A JUDGMENT BY DEFAULT MAY BE TAKEN AGAINST YOU FOR THE RELIEF ASKED IN THE COMPLAINT.

To the officer:

This summons must be returned by the officer or other person to whom it was given for service, with indorsement of service and fees, if any, immediately after service and not less than 3 days before the day for appearance. If service cannot be made, this summons shall be returned so indorsed. This summons may not be served later than 3 days before the day for appearance.

(Seal of Court)   Witness _____ , 19 _____

                              _____
                              (Clerk of the Court)

Plaintiff _____   City _____

Address _____   Phone _____

Praecipe

STATE OF _____
IN THE CIRCUIT COURT OF THE _____ JUDICIAL CIRCUIT
COUNTY OF _____

_____
Plaintiff

v.   Case No. _____

_____
Defendant

PRAECIPE FOR SERVICE OF SUMMONS

Please issue summons in the above cause to the Sheriff of
_____ County, _____ , to be served
on the following:

Name of Defendant(s): _____

_____

Address of Defendant(s): _____

_____

Work Address: _____

_____

Plaintiff _____

Special instructions for service: _____

_____

_____

Motion For Private Process Service

STATE OF _____
IN THE CIRCUIT COURT OF THE _____ JUDICIAL CIRCUIT
COUNTY OF _____

MOTION FOR LEAVE TO USE PRIVATE PROCESS

COMES NOW the Plaintiff, _____
and moves the Court pursuant to state law for leave to serve the
Defendant(s) in this cause by private process through
_____ , and states as grounds
therefore the following:

(1) Plaintiff retains _____ as its
private process server throughout the state of _____
_____ , which substantially reduces the cost of this
action and, ultimately, the cost to Defendant(s) upon judgment;

(2) Service of process will not prejudice the rights of
Defendant(s) in any manner;

(3) Private process will be in the best interests of justice
and will relieve additional burden of this court.

_____
Plaintiff

Plaintiff _____

Address _____

City _____

Telephone _____

Order For Private Process Service

STATE OF _____
IN THE CIRCUIT COURT OF THE _____ JUDICIAL CIRCUIT
COUNTY OF _____

ORDER GRANTING LEAVE TO USE PRIVATE PROCESS

UPON Plaintiff's motion, and the Court being otherwise fully advised;

Now therefore, it is hereby ORDERED that Plaintiff be granted leave to serve the Defendant(s) by private process through _____ , an employee of _____ .

Entered: _____

_____
              Judge

Plaintiff _____

Address _____

City _____

Telephone _____

Post-Judgment Letter

May 19, 199_

Mr. Richard Landwert
Landwert Movers and Haulers
111 W. Main
Phoenix, FL 31101

Re: Brown Enterprises v. Landwert Movers and Haulers

Dear Mr. Landwert,

Unless I receive your immediate cooperation in making a payment arrangement on the judgment which has been entered against you, I will have no alternative but to proceed with further legal action. This may include a Subpoena to determine your assets and liabilities. You will be forced to produce all records requested and appear at a designated time and place for this examination. Other alternatives include garnishments, both of wages and bank accounts.

If you wish to avoid further legal action, please contact me at once at _____ . Please contact me by ___(7 days from now)___ . Thank you for your attention to this matter.

Sincerely,

Nancy Brown, C.E.O.

Brown Enterprises

Entry of Appearance, Stipulation for Judgment

STATE OF _____

IN THE CIRCUIT COURT OF THE _____ JUDICIAL CIRCUIT

COUNTY OF _____

(You, d/b/a
Your Business)

Plaintiff

        v.   Case No. _____

(John D. Debtor)
Defendant

ENTRY OF APPEARANCE, STIPULATION FOR JUDGMENT

Plaintiff and Defendant each enter their appearance herein, waive service of process, and stipulate that this Court enters judgment against Defendant for Plaintiff in the amount of $ _____ plus the cost of this suit.

_____
Plaintiff

_____
Defendant

Subscribed and Sworn to before me

_____ , 199_ .

_____
Notary Public

Affidavit For Wage Deduction Order

STATE OF _____
IN THE CIRCUIT COURT OF THE _____ JUDICIAL CIRCUIT
COUNTY OF _____

_____
Plaintiff

      v.   Case No. _____

_____
Defendant

AFFIDAVIT FOR WAGE DEDUCTION ORDER

_____ on oath states:

1. Judgment was entered in this case on _____ , 19 ____ , in favor of judgment creditor _____ and against judgment debtor for $ _____ and costs.

2. $ _____ has been paid on the judgment.

3. There is unpaid on the judgment:

$ _____ principal

$ _____ costs

$ _____ interest

$ _____ TOTAL

4. I believe employer _____ is or will be indebted to the judgment debtor for wages due or to become due.

5. The lasts known address of the judgment debtor is: _____
_____

I request that summons be issued and directed to the employer.

_____
Plaintiff

Signed and sworn to before me

_____,19 ___ .

_____
Notary Public

- -

Plaintiff _____

Address_____

City _____

Telephone _____

Wage Deduction Summons

STATE OF _____
IN THE CIRCUIT COURT OF THE _____ JUDICIAL CIRCUIT
COUNTY OF _____

_____

Plaintiff

v.   Case No. _____

_____

Defendant

WAGE DEDUCTION SUMMONS

TO THE EMPLOYER:

YOU ARE SUMMONED and required to file answers to the judgment creditor's interrogatories, in the Office of the Clerk of this Court at the Courthouse, _____(City) _____ , ___ (State)___, on _____ or before _____ , 19___ .

However, if this summons is served on you less than 56 days before that date, you must file answers to the interrogatories on or before a new return date, to be set by the court, not less than 56 days after you were served with this summons.

You must not file your answers to the interrogatories sooner than 56 days after service of this summons. This proceeding applies to non-exempt wages due at the time you were served with this summons and to wages which become due until the expiration of your payroll period ending immediately prior to 56 days after you were served with this summons.

IF YOU FAIL TO ANSWER, A CONDITIONAL JUDGMENT BY DEFAULT MAY BE TAKEN AGAINST YOU FOR THE AMOUNT OF THE JUDGMENT UNPAID.

To the officer:

This summons must be returned by the officer or other person to whom to was given for service, with indorsement of service and fees, if any, immediately after service. If service cannot be made, this summons shall be returned so indorsed. This summons may not be served later than the above date.

Witness _____ , 19_____

_____
(Clerk of the Court)

(Seal of Court)   By:_____
                              (Deputy)

Plaintiff _____

Address _____

City _____

Telephone _____

Affidavit For Garnishment—Non-Wage

STATE OF _____

IN THE CIRCUIT COURT OF THE _____ JUDICIAL CIRCUIT

COUNTY OF _____

_____

Plaintiff

v.   Case No. _____

_____

Defendant

AFFIDAVIT FOR GARNISHMENT—NON-WAGE

_____ on oath states:

1.   Judgment was entered in this case on _____ , 19 _____ , in favor of judgment creditor _____ and against judgment debtor for $ _____ and costs.

2. $ _____ has been paid on the judgment.

3.   There is unpaid on the judgment:

    $ _____ principal

    $ _____ costs

    $ _____ interest

    $ _____ TOTAL

4.   I believe garnishee _____ is indebted to the judgment debtor or has in his possesion, custody or control property belonging to him or in which he has an interest. I request that summons be issued and directed to the garnishee

                              _____
                              Plaintiff

Signed and sworn to before me

_____ ,19 ____ .

_____

Notary Public

Plaintiff _____

Address_____

City _____

Telephone _____

Garnishment Summons—Non-Wage

STATE OF _____

IN THE CIRCUIT COURT OF THE _____ JUDICIAL CIRCUIT

COUNTY OF _____

_____

Plaintiff

　　　　　　　v. 　　　　　　　　　　　　　Case No. _____

_____

Defendant

WAGE DEDUCTION SUMMONS

TO THE EMPLOYER:

YOU ARE SUMMONED and required to file answers to the judgment creditor's interrogatories, in the Office of the Clerk of this Court at the Courthouse, _____ (City) _____ , _____ (State) _____ , on _____ or before _____ , 19 __ .

However, if this summons is served on you less than 10 days before that date, you must file answers to the interrogatories on or before 14 days after that date.

IF YOU FAIL TO DO SO, A CONDITIONAL JUDGMENT BY DEFAULT MAY BE TAKEN AGAINST YOU FOR THE AMOUNT OF THE JUDGMENT UNPAID.

To the officer:

This summons must be returned by the officer or other person to whom to was given for service, with indorsement of service and fees, if any, immediately after service. If service cannot be made, this summons shall be returned so indorsed. This summons may not be served later than the above date.

Witness _____ , 19 _____

_____

(Clerk of the Court)

(Seal of Court)　　　　By: _____

(Deputy)

Plaintiff _____

Address _____

City _____

Phone _____

Subpoena

STATE OF _____
IN THE CIRCUIT COURT OF THE _____ JUDICIAL CIRCUIT
COUNTY OF _____

_____

Plaintiff

        v.   Case No. _____

_____

Defendant

SUBPOENA

TO:

YOU ARE COMMANDED to appear before the Circuit Court at _____ on _____ , 19 ____ at _____ _____ m. to be examined under oath concerning the property or income of, or indebtedness due _____ . Judgment was entered on _____ , 19 _____ . $ _____ remains unsatisfied.

YOU ARE COMMANDED to produce at the examination:

and all books, papers or records in your possession or control which may contain information concerning the property or income of, or indebtedness due judgment debtor.

YOU ARE PROHIBITED from making or allowing any transfer or other disposition of, or interfering with, any property not exempt from execution or garnishment belonging to the judgment debtor or to which he may be entitled or which may be acquired by or become due to him, until the further order of court or termination of the proceedings. You are not required to withhold the payment of any money beyond double the amount of the judgment.

YOUR FAILURE TO COMPLY WITH THIS CITATION MAY SUBJECT YOU TO PUNISHMENT FOR CONTEMPT OF THIS COURT OR TO A JUDGMENT FOR THE AMOUNT UNPAID.

Witness _____ , 19_____
(Clerk of the Court)

Name _____

Address _____

City _____

Telephone _____

(Seal of Court)

Date of Service _____

Affidavit of Assets and Liabilities

I, _____ , defendant in this case, on oath state the following:

Name _____ Date of Birth _____

Address_____ Phone _____

City_____ State _____

Place of Employment _____

Length of Employment_____ Occupation _____

Spouse's name _____

Spouse's Place of Employment _____

Length of Employment_____ Occupation _____

Earnings:

_____ per month from employment _____ per month from pension, trusts, welfare, workman's compensation, retirement, disability, or any state, federal, local or private benefit plan.

_____ per month from other sources

Assets: Home or other dwelling $ _____

Address: _____

Car $ _____ Make_____ Year_____

Checking Acct $ _____ Bank _____

Savings Acct $ _____ Bank _____

Other Assets _____

I offer to pay $ _____ per month, beginning _____ , 199_ .

I certify the foregoing is true to the best of my knowledge and belief.

_____
(Signature)

Signed and sworn to before me

_____ ,19_ .

_____
Notary Public

STATE BAR ASSOCIATIONS

The state bar associations should be able to point you in the correct direction with general information, addresses, and phone numbers for the clerk's office in each county in each state in the United States.

General Requests:

American Bar Association
750 N. Lakeshore Dr.
Chicago, Illinois 60611
(800) 621-6159
(312) 988-5000

State Bar Associations:

Alabama State Bar
415 Dexter Street
P.O. Box 671
Montgomery, Alabama 36104
(205) 269-1515

Alaska Bar Association
310 K Street, No. 602
P.O. Box 100279
Anchorage, Alaska 99501
(907) 272-7469

State Bar of Arizona
363 N. 1st Ave.
Phoenix, Arizona 85003
(602) 252-4804

Arkansas Bar Association
400 W. Markham
Little Rock, Arkansas 72201
(501) 375-4605

State Bar of California
555 Franklin Street
San Francisco, California 94102
(415) 561-8200
(415) 561-8228 (Fax)

Colorado Bar Association
No. 950, 1990 Grant Street
Denver, Colorado 80203
(303) 860-1115
(303) 894-0821 (Fax)

Connecticut Bar Association
101 Corporate Place
Rocky Hill, Connecticut 06067
(203) 721-0025
(203) 257-4125 (Fax)

Delaware Bar Association
708 Market Street
Wilmington, Delaware 19899
(302) 658-5278

District of Columbia Bar
6th Floor
1707 L. Street, N.W.
Washington, D.C. 20036
(202) 331-3883
(202) 223-7726 (Fax)

Bar Association of the District of Columbia
12th Floor
1819 H. Street, N.W.
Washington, D.C. 20006
(202) 223-6600
(202) 293-3383 (Fax)

The Florida Bar
The Florida Bar Center
650 Apalachee Parkway
Tallahassee, Florida 32399-2300
(904) 561-5600
(904) 222-3729 (Fax)

State Bar of Georgia
800 The Hurt Building
50 Hurt Plaza
Atlanta, Georgia 30303
(404) 527-8700
(404) 527-8717 (Fax)

Hawaii State Bar Association
Suite 950 Pacific Tower
1001 Bishop Street
Honolulu, Hawaii 96813
(808) 537-1868

Idaho State Bar
P.O. Box 895
Boise, Idaho 83701
(208) 342-8958

Illinois State Bar Association
424 South Second Street
Springfield, Illinois 62701
(217) 525-1760
(217) 525-0712 (Fax)

Indiana State Bar Association
6th Floor
230 East Ohio Street
Indianapolis, Indiana 46204
(317) 639-5465

Iowa State Bar Association
110 Fleming Building
Des Moines, Iowa 50309
(515) 243-3179
(515) 243-2511 (Fax)

Kansas Bar Association
1200 Harrison Street
Topeka, Kansas 66612
(913) 234-5696
(913) 234-3813 (Fax)

Kentucky Bar Association
West Main at Kentucky River
Frankfort, Kentucky 40601
(502) 564-3795

Louisiana State Bar Association
601 St. Charles Avenue
New Orleans, Louisiana 70130
(504) 566-1600
(504) 566-0930 (Fax)

Maine State Bar Association
124 State Street
P.O. Box 788
Augusta, Maine 04330
(207) 622-7523
(207) 623-4140 (Fax)

Maryland State Bar Association, Inc.
520 West Fayette Street
Baltimore, Maryland 21201
(301) 685-7878
(301) 837-0518 (Fax)

Massachusetts Bar Association
20 West Street
Boston, Massachusetts 02111
(617) 542-3602
(617) 426-4344 (Fax)

State Bar of Michigan
306 Townsend Street
Lansing, Michigan 48933-2083
(517) 372-9030
(517) 482-6248 (Fax)

Minnesota State Bar Association
Suite 403
430 Marquette Avenue
Minneapolis, Minnesota 55401
(612) 333-1183
(612) 333-4927 (Fax)

Mississippi State Bar
643 N. State Street
Jackson, Mississippi 39202
(601) 948-4471

The Missouri Bar
326 Monroe
Jefferson City, Missouri 65102
(314) 635-4128
(314) 635-2811 (Fax)

State Bar of Montana
46 North Last Chance Gulch, Suite 2A
P.O. Box 577
Helena, Montana 59624
(406) 442-7660
(406) 442-7763 (Fax)

Nebraska State Bar Association
635 South 14th Street
Lincoln, Nebraska 68508
(402) 475-7091
(402) 475-7098 (Fax)

State Bar of Nevada
Suite 2
295 Holcomb Avenue
Reno, Nevada 89502-1085
(702) 382-0502
(702) 329-0522 (Fax)

New Hampshire Bar Association
112 Pleasant Street
Concord, New Hampshire 03301
(603) 224-6942
(603) 224-2910 (Fax)

New Jersey State Bar Association
One Constitution Square
New Brunswick, New Jersey 08901-1500
(201) 249-5000
(201) 249-2815 (Fax)

State Bar of New Mexico
121 Tijeras Street, N.E.
Albuquerque, New Mexico 87102
(505) 842-6132
(505) 843-8765 (Fax)

New York State Bar Association
One Elk Street
Albany, New York 12207
(518) 463-3200
(518) 463-4276 (Fax)

North Carolina State Bar
208 Fayetteville Street Mall
Raleigh, North Carolina 27611
(919) 828-4620

North Carolina Bar Association
1312 Annapolis Drive
P.O. Box 12806
Raleigh, North Carolina 27611
(919) 828-0561

State Bar Association of North Dakota
Suite 101
515 1/2 East Broadway
Bismark, North Dakota 58501
(701) 255-1404
(701) 224-1621 (Fax)

Ohio State Bar Association
33 West Eleventh Avenue
Columbus, Ohio 43201
(614) 487-2050
(614) 487-1008 (Fax)

Oklahoma Bar Association
1901 North Lincoln
Oklahoma City, Oklahoma 73105
(405) 524-2365
(405) 524-1115 (Fax)

Oregon State Bar
5200 S.W. Meadows Road
P.O. Box 1689
Lake Oswego, Oregon 97035
(503) 620-0222
(503) 684-1366 (Fax)

Pennsylvania Bar Association
100 South Street
P.O. Box 186
Harrisburg, Pennsylvania 17108
(717) 238-6715
(717) 238-1204 (Fax)

Puerto Rico Bar Association
P.O. Box 1900
San Juan, Puerto Rico 00903
(809) 721-3358

Rhode Island Bar Association
91 Friendship Street
Providence, Rhode Island 02903
(401) 421-5740

South Carolina Bar
950 Taylor Street
P.O. Box 608
Columbia, South Carolina 29202
(803) 799-6653

State Bar of South Dakota
222 East Capitol
Pierre, South Dakota 57501
(605) 224-7554

Tennessee Bar Association
3622 Westend Avenue
Nashville, Tennessee 37205
(615) 383-7421

State Bar of Texas
1414 Colorado
P.O. Box 12487
Austin, Texas 78711
(512) 463-1463

Utah State Bar
645 S. 200 East
Salt Lake City, Utah 84111
(801) 531-9077
(801) 531-0660 (Fax)

Vermont Bar Association
P.O. Box 100
Montpelier, Vermont 05602
(802) 223-2020

Virgin Islands Bar Association
46 King Street
Christiansted, Virgin Islands 00822
(809) 778-7497

Virginia State Bar
Suite 1000, Ross Building
801 East Main Street
Richmond, Virginia 23219
(804) 786-2061
(703) 786-3036 (Fax)

Virginia Bar Association
Suite 1515
701 East Franklin Street
Richmond, Virginia 23219
(804) 644-0041
(804) 644-0052 (Fax)

Washington State Bar Association
500 Westin Building
2001 Sixth Avenue
Seattle, Washington 98121-2599
(206) 448-0441

West Virginia State Bar
E-400 State Capitol
Charleston, West Virginia 25305
(304) 346-8414
(304) 348-2467 (Fax)

West Virginia Bar Association
904 Security Building
100 Capitol Street
Charleston, West Virginia 25301
(304) 342-1474

State Bar of Wisconsin
402 West Wilson Street
Madison, Wisconsin 53703
(608) 257-3838
(608) 257-5502 (Fax)

Wyoming State Bar
500 Randall Avenue
Cheyenne, Wyoming 82001
(307) 632-9061
(307) 632-3737 (Fax)

Appendix C

GLOSSARY

APPEAL: The act of taking your claim, once a judgment is made at the lower court, to the next higher court for another determination.

ATTACHMENT: The act of having the sheriff collect goods owned by a person who owes you money from a judgment.

BANKRUPTCY: The act of wiping away your debts (an all too common practice in the 1990s). An individual may go through this process every seven years. A bankruptcy will stay on credit reports for approximately ten years.

CITATION TO DISCOVER ASSETS: A court hearing after you have received a judgment where the debtor is required to answer your questions as to his assets and liabilities and how he plans to pay the judgment.

CLAIM: A demand that someone owes you money or property.

CLERK: A public servant whose work at the courthouse includes filing court documents and keeping court records.

COMPLAINT: The first document filed with the court in a small claims proceeding. This document will typically list the plaintiff and defendant, the reason the plaintiff is suing, and the dollar amount.

CONTEMPT: A proceeding or an order from the judge saying that an individual has not followed the judge's orders. A criminal charge that may have serious consequences, i.e., jail.

CONTINUANCE: The adjournment or postponement to a subsequent date of an action pending in a court.

CREDITOR: Synonymous with plaintiff. The individual who is owed money by another.

DAMAGES: The dollar amount you are claiming.

DEBTOR: Synonymous with defendant. The individual who owes money to someone else.

DEFENDANT: The individual who is being sued.

DEMAND LETTER: A letter sent by a creditor to the debtor requesting payment on the debt.

DEPOSITION IN AID OF EXECUTION: A proceeding after a judgment is received. An investigation of the debtor under oath to determine a debtor's assets and liabilities.

DISPOSABLE INCOME: Net income. Amount of income after taxes and court ordered deductions, such as alimony, are taken out.

DISTRESS OF RENT: When a landlord sues to get the amount of rent owed to him, but is not trying to evict the tenant.

EXTENSION: The judge may grant additional time to either party so that they have more time to prepare their case.

FILING FEE: The amount you have to pay the court in order to start the proceedings. You must pay the fee when you file the lawsuit.

FILING SUIT: The act of giving the complaint, summons, and filing fee to the court clerk, getting a case number, and, quite probably, a court date.

FORCIBLE ENTRY AND DETAINER: The procedure by which a landlord evicts a tenant from his or her property and obtains a judgment for back rent and/or property damage.

GARNISHMENT: The act of taking the debtor's property toward satisfaction of the judgment, whether it be wages, bank accounts, stocks, or bonds.

HEARING: The first time you will meet the judge. At this meeting, both sides will tell their side of the story. Depending on the court, the judge will either make a determination at this time or set a new date for a formal trial.

HOMESTEAD EXEMPTION: Most states protect homeowners to some extent from judgments and creditors. Some or all of their property may be exempt from most court actions.

INJURY: How you have been wronged. What it is that has been broken and needs fixed. *See also* damages.

JUDGMENT: An order given by the judge that one party has won the case.

JUDGMENT LIEN: A document that is either automatically or manually filed with the clerk stating that a person is indebted to you for a certain amount of money.

JURISDICTION: Whether the court has the power or ability to hear a particular dispute. This depends on many things, including the type of dispute, the dollar amount contested, where the dispute arose, and the citizenship of the parties.

LAWSUIT: The legal proceeding which results from one person suing another.

LESSEE: The person who rents real property, such as an apartment or house, or personal property, such as a car or home furnishings.

LESSOR: The person who owns and rents out to another any form of real property, such as an apartment or house, or personal property, such as a car or home furnishings.

LEVY: The act of getting the property of a debtor, typically after a judgment.

LIABILITY: Whether someone actually owes you money under the law for their actions or nonactions.

LIEN: An obligation that hangs over property until the judgment is paid off.

LIEN ON REAL ESTATE: A document that is either automatically or manually filed with the clerk stating that a person is indebted to you for a certain amount of money. The property cannot be sold until the lien is first paid off.

NEGLIGENCE: When the actions of someone are wrong in the eyes of the law.

PERSONAL PROPERTY: Any property other than real estate.

PLAINTIFF: The person doing the suing.

PLEADING: Another name for the documents filed with the court.

PRIVATE PROCESS SERVER: A person appointed by the court to deliver court documents to parties to the case.

REAL PROPERTY: Real estate.

RULE TO SHOW CAUSE: Also called a contempt proceeding. *See also* contempt.

SECURED DEBT: Any obligation guaranteed by collateral of either real or personal property.

SERVICE OF PROCESS: The act of delivering the court documents to the other party in the action. This may be by certified mail, sheriff, or a private process server.

SMALL CLAIMS: A special department in the courthouse which deals exclusively with small civil actions, typically below $5,000.

STATEMENT OF CLAIM: Synonymous with complaint. *See also* complaint.

STATUTE OF LIMITATION: The time period allowed by the state law as to the maximum time allowed between the time a debtor fails to pay you money and the time you sue the debtor.

SUBPOENA: A court document typically delivered by the sheriff demanding a person to appear before the court at a certain date and time.

THEORY OF THE CASE: An explanation of what happened to cause the problem between the plaintiff and the defendant. The explanation of why it is that the plaintiff thinks the defendant owes the money. Each side has a story, or theory of the case.

TORT: A civil wrong or injury.

TRIAL: A more formal hearing. You will be expected to have your witnesses, testimony, and other evidence in order for this court appearance.

UNSECURED DEBT: An obligation not guaranteed by any form of collateral.

VENUE: The proper court(s) where you can sue an individual or business.

WAGE GARNISHMENT: Used after a judgment is received. The creditor can use this to attach a percentage of the debtor's wages for a certain time period or until the judgment is paid off.

WITNESS: A person who is familiar with the facts and history of your case who is brought to court to be examined before the judge.

WRIT OF EXECUTION: Used after a judgment is received. A document that is prepared by you, filed with the clerk, and given to the sheriff to serve on the defendant. It is an order to the sheriff to pick up certain property or possessions of the defendant and hand them over to you or sell them at a Sheriff's Auction and give you the proceeds.

About Sourcebooks Trade

In 1990, Sourcebooks Inc., started its trade division, Sourcebooks Trade. Our goal was to provide easy-to-understand, empowering how-to books for today's consumers. We began by developing practical business and finance books. Offering a wide range of expertise, we now also include titles in the areas of marketing, current affairs, self-help and reference designed to make consumers' lives easier. **Our Sourcebooks Trade Titles include:**

The Basics of Finance: Financial Tools for Non-Financial Managers
by Bryan E. Milling

Ideal for every businessperson without a financial background who now aspires to management responsibility. Written in readable language, *The Basics of Finance* offers tools to help non-financial managers master financial information including understanding annual reports, interacting with financial personnel and using financial analysis to better understand the business world. It features 31 fundamental principles of financial management clearly and concisely explained, and includes simplified case histories illustrating each principle.

A selection of The Business Week Book Club and The Newbridge Executive Program.

The Basics of Finance is an essential desk companion for any manager with direct or indirect financial responsibility ... and a key tool for professionals aspiring to the corner office.

210 pages   ISBN 0-942061-18-7 (paperback) $14.95
ISBN 0-942061-25-X (hardcover) $24.95

Cash Flow Problem Solver: Common Problems and Practical Solutions
by Bryan E. Milling

Thousands of business owners have discovered that the *Cash Flow Problem Solver: Common Problems and Practical Solutions* is a tool of surpassing value in the day-to-day management of a firm's cash flow. Now in its third edition, *Cash Flow Problem Solver* is a proven bestseller and has helped over 20,000 business owners **improve their cash flow and benefit from effective cash flow management.**

Cited as one of the three books on the "Smart CEO's Reading List" in INC Magazine. Selected as an alternate of both the **Business Week Book Club** and the **Fortune Book Club.** *Cash Flow Problem Solver: Common Problems and Practical Solutions* is a profits-oriented approach to cash flow management. In addition, *Cash Flow Problem Solver* **provides a results-oriented, step-by-step guide with tools and specific tactics to assure positive cash flow and to help boost a firm's profits.**

296 pages ISBN 0-942061-27-6 (paperback) $19.95
0-942061-28-4   (hardcover) $32.95

Creating Your Own Future: A Woman's Guide to Retirement Planning
by Judith A. Martindale, CFP and Mary J. Moses

Planning your future can be a wonderful and trying experience all at the same time. As authors, Judith Martindale and Mary Moses found, creating a simple, more relaxed and enjoyable retirement takes patience and hard work. "Critical decisions must be made well in advance to turn a dream into a comfortable reality," say Martindale and Moses.

The authors argue that although retirement planning is important to everyone, factors unique to women, such as, shorter work lives due to child rearing, longer life expectancy, differing health needs than men, among others, make appropriate preparations essential.

The first book on retirement planning for women. 85% of women will face retirement alone. *Creating Your Own Future* provides: step-by-step procedures to help women evaluate their current financial position; easy-to-follow instructions, tables and worksheets for effective planning; complete explanations of Social Security benefits, Medicare, pensions and profit-sharing funds; and advice on being an active participant in a spouse's retirement package.

"The crucial work on women and how they relate to money on all levels...emotional, practical and psychological." —*Focus on Books*. "Highly recommended."—*Booklist*

256 pages ISBN 0-942061-09-8 (paperback) $14.95
0-942061-08-X (hardcover) $28.95

Finding Time: Breathing Space For Women Who Do Too Much
by Paula Peisner

Finding Time: Breathing Space For Women Who Do Too Much is a terrific book for today's women who always seem to be doing more than they have time to do. Balancing careers, families, homes, and outside interests, women are feeling out of control and stressed.

This book is for all women who want to take control of their own time and make more of it. The book shows women how to identify and eliminate actions by themselves and others that rob them of their most precious asset... time.

"Comprehensive and insightful - easy tips to understand.
Taking even a few of these tips to heart should allow some breathing space."
— Sandra N. Bane, Partner
KPMG Peat Marwick

"Provides a wonderful insight into a working woman's management of time.
A very practical primer. I found it very useful."
— Anita R. Gershman, President and CEO
World International Network

256 pages ISBN 0-942061-33-0 (paperback) $ 7.95
ISBN 0-942061-35-7 (hardcover) $16.95

Future Vision: The 189 Most Important Trends of the 1990s
From the Editors of Research Alert

". . . the ultimate guide to the new decade."—*American Demographics*

". . . a valuable tool and a bargain."—*Media Industry Newsletter*

". . . a stunningly complete summary."—*Executive Trend Watch*

". . . especially useful."—Robert Tuefel, President, Rodale Press

Future Vision gives substance to the dynamically changing forces that are reshaping the American marketplace. Its unique presentation of both the facts and the fictions presents readers with an evenhanded perspective of what will happen next. . . with enough detail for them to see the implications of their own work.

". . . a wealth of information"
—Adweek's Marketing Week

Presented in a usable, readable format, this guide examines key trends in areas including: Money, Media, Home, Leisure, Food, Environmentalism and the Workplace. No outdated trends or thinking . . just the cutting-edge numbers drawn from hundreds of sources. A special selection of the Newbridge Book Clubs.

256 pages ISBN 0-942061-16-0 (paperback) $12.95
0-942061-17-9 (hardcover) $21.95

The Lifestyle Odyssey:
The Facts Behind the Social, Personal and Cultural Changes Touching Each of Our Lives. . .
From the Way We Eat Our Cookies to Our Desire for a Better World
from the Editors of Research Alert

The Lifestyle Odyssey touches all social and cultural changes affecting our American lifestyle it takes us on a journey — a pathway describing a new American lifestyle. Beyond the obvious demographic shifts, American society is changing the way it chooses to live. The cumulative effect of those choices will give way to a "new" American lifestyle. All of us have experienced these changes to some extent. *The Lifestyle Odyssey* crystallizes the loose feelings that these changes have engendered in many Americans and outlines what else we may expect.

"Whatever your profession or personal investment program,
somewhere in this remarkable new book lurks a fact or a trend that will change
what you do. **If you have but one life to live, read this book."**
John Mack Carter,
editor-in-chief of
Good Housekeeping Magazine.

304 pages ISBN 0-942061-36-5 (paperback) $15.95

Small Claims Court Without A Lawyer
by W. Kelsea Wilber, Attorney-at-Law

Small Claims Court Without A Lawyer is an invaluable guide to understanding the small claims system. It allows you to file a claim and get a judgement quickly and ecomomically, without an attorney's assistance or fee. Written in clear, uncomplicated language, this useful new book includes details about each state's small claims court system, so that wherever you live you can use it to successfully file a claim and see that claim through to a judgement.

"An excellent primer for individuals or small businesses attempting to collect their own debts." — Arthur G. Sartorius, III, Attorney-at-Law.

**"A good basic guide for individuals and small businesses;
explains a complicated process in easy to understand steps.
A copy will be made a permanent part of our business assistance library and its purchase has
already been recommended to some of our clients with collection problems."**
— Bill Larson, Business Analyst,
University of North Florida,
Small Business Development Center

"The easy-to-read format is comprehensive but offers the basics necessary for the non-lawyer to proceed and succeed!" —Drew W. Prusiecki, Attorney-at-Law

224 pages   ISBN 0-942061-32-2 (paperback) $18.95

To order these books or any of our numerous other publications, **please contact your local bookseller.**

You can also obtain a copy of our catalog by writing or faxing:
Sourcebooks Trade
A Div. of Sourcebooks, Inc.
P.O. Box 372
Naperville, IL 60566

or call Sourcebooks at: (708) 961-2161
FAX: 708-961-2168

Thank you for your interest in our publications.